The Making of America

HOW THE SCOTS-IRISH SHAPED A NATION

Best wishes
Billy Kennedy

by
BILLY KENNEDY

AMBASSADOR

BELFAST, NORTHERN IRELAND
GREENVILLE, SOUTH CAROLINA

The Making of America
© 2001 Billy Kennedy
ISBN 1 84030 109 0
First published September, 2001

PRINTED IN NORTHERN IRELAND

Published by
Causeway Press
an imprint of
Ambassador Productions Ltd.,
Providence House
Ardenlee Street,
Belfast, BT6 8QJ
www.ambassador-productions.com

Emerald House Group Inc.
427 Wade Hampton Boulevard,
Greenville,
South Carolina 29609
www.emeraldhouse.com

About *the Author*

THIS SEVENTH BOOK in seven years in the popular series of Scots-Irish Chronicles by Northern Ireland journalist and author Billy Kennedy reveals more of the absorbing story of the hardy 18th century settlers from the Irish province of Ulster who moved on to the American frontier in big numbers and created a civilisation out of a wilderness. Billy Kennedy, who lives in Co Armagh, has been a leading Northern Ireland journalist for the past 30 years, occupying the roles of news editor, assistant editor and leader writer with the Belfast News Letter, the main morning newspaper in Northern Ireland founded in 1737, in a career which spanned 1974-1998. He is now a freelance journalist, author and public relations consultant, combining news, features, business and sports coverage in Northern Ireland for national press and media outlets in the United Kingdom and the Republic of Ireland. On his regular visits to the United States, he lectures on the subject of the Scots-Irish diaspora at universities, colleges, historical and genealogical societies and public authorities in cities and towns of the south eastern American states. His other interests are sport and American country music. He is married with a grown-up daughter.

List *of contents*

Foreword *from the United States*

Dr. John Rice Irwin

Adocument drawn up by a small group of men in a remote and largely unpopulated colony of the mighty British Empire is often referred to as "the greatest document in human history". It is remarkable, indeed, that this dissident group in the American colonies should even consider defying what was then the world's greatest empire.

It is even more unlikely that these few souls would also succeed in playing a dominant role in formulating this Declaration of Independence. It is remarkable, too, that the driving force of colonialists behind the Declaration and the subsequent defeat of the British in the Revolutionary War was a small group of stalwarts from the north of Ireland, or the Irish province of Ulster - today Northern Ireland, an area scarcely larger than a dot on the world's map.

These were the Scots-Irish Presbyterians whose ancestors had migrated from Scotland to Ireland and, eventually, to North America,

The respected philosopher and writer Colonel A. K. McClure said: "It was the Scots-Irish people in the colonies who made the American Declaration of Independence in 1776."

The Scots-Irish in the American colonies were the first to come forward when the Revolutionary War started. And they were considered to be among the most dedicated and effective warriors during this conflict for independence.

Who were these folk who played such an important part in the establishment of what would become the most respected and powerful nation in the world? Well, Billy Kennedy, the prolific writer from Northern Ireland, has again addressed the subject.

In 1995, Billy wrote about the late 18th century Scots-Irish frontier pioneers in Tennessee and, in 1996, about the important influence of this hardy breed of people in the settlements and development of the beautifully and strategically important Shenandoah Valley of Virginia.

The response from the public, both in the United States, and in the United Kingdom where Billy Kennedy resides, was very positive in arousing interest in these folk, and in titillating people in America to look deeper and more substantively into the culture and history of the Scots-Irish.

These warmly received works inspired Billy Kennedy to write another book on the Scots-Irish in the Carolinas; and another on the Scots-Irish in Pennsylvania and Kentucky. His other books were Faith and Freedom, the story of how the religion of the Scots-Irish helped shape life in America, and Heroes of the Scots-Irish, which featured some of the most revered names in American history. With this latest publication, he now has published seven books on the outstanding contribution these colourful and resolute Scots-Irish have made to various geographical settlements in the United States.

Every time Billy Kennedy has written a book he has honoured me with a request that I should write a foreword, and every time I thought it would be the last. And now he has sallied forth with this interesting and deeply fascinating story of how a tiny group of dedicated souls from a tiny race on this earth, so profound and so permanently, effected the birth of this nation.

The careful and human-interest references, to the various individuals and to their respective and collective roles in gaining our independence from Great Britain, is bound to spark and rekindle the pursuit of this story more in depth.

Billy Kennedy says that this is his last book, but he said that six times before!

DR JOHN RICE IRWIN,
Director of Museum of Appalachia, Norris, Tennessee

• **DR JOHN RICE IRWIN** is founder and director of the Museum of Appalachia at Norris, Tennessee, 15 miles from the city of Knoxville. Dr Irwin has been a teacher, farmer, businessman, historian, author and his wide range of interests extends to the music of the south eastern Appalachian region. His family is of Scots-Irish and Welsh origin.

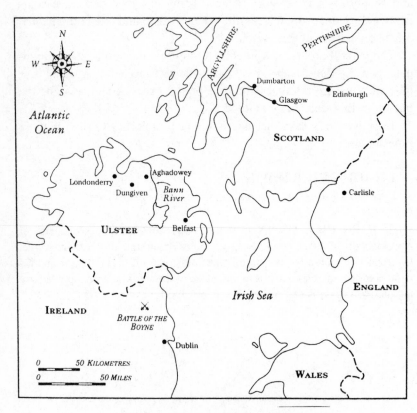

England, Scotland, Wales and Ireland.

Foreword *from Northern Ireland*

Lord Laird of Artigarvan

This is the latest in a most excellent series of books by the Ulster historian and journalist Billy Kennedy. It provides an amazing and clear insight into the 18th century and early 19th century melting pot of the emerging United States. The particular activity that the author examines in some detail is the quite considerable role played by the Ulster-Scots or Scots-Irish community.

Few groups of people from such a small area have contributed more to the development of the modern world than the Scots-Irish. With their harsh experiences at the hands of church and state in both Scotland and Ireland, the many who emigrated to the new world took with them the burning desire to create a better and more just society.

Fashioned by events and possessing a passionate belief in "their right arms" and the commitment to learn the lessons of history, the Scots-Irish were ideal frontiersmen and architects for a new land.

New arrivals, or as members of the first and second generations of Americans, the Scots-Irish were undaunted by the formidable odds that nearly always seemed stacked against them. Their involvement in the War of Independence and the creation of the institutions of the emerging United States was key.

Many of the major names of the Revolutionary War period as detailed by Billy Kennedy were of Scots-Irish Presbyterian stock. One of the most pleasing aspects of recent years has been the increasing recognition, on both sides of the Atlantic, of the Scots-Irish culture and its role and importance to modern history.

In their recognition, a major contribution has been the part played by Billy Kennedy. This publication is a most important contribution to that tremendous story.

THE LORD LAIRD of ARTIGARVAN.

• **LORD LAIRD of ARTIGARVAN** is chairman of the Ulster-Scots Agency in Belfast, Northern Ireland and a member of the House of Lords at Westminster in London. He is a former Northern Ireland Member of Parliament and is head of a public relations company in Belfast.

1

Without the Scots-Irish
independence would have been a fancy

The Scots-Irish during the American Revolutionary War of the 1770s and 1780s were acknowledged as the most effective element in George Washington's patriot army. They were also highly influential in the Continental Congress which ran America during the War from its Pennsylvania base, and in the various colonial assemblies, from the eastern seaboard region to the Appalachian frontier lands to the west.

The Scots-Irish - in the Continental Congress, the army and in the colonies - were indeed the activists, the intelligencia and, in the ranks of the backwoods militias, the resolute and uncompromising champions of the movement for independence in America.

A minority of the Scots-Irish settlers in the American colonies remained loyal to the British Crown, but up to eighty per cent of these people were persuaded that their interests were best served by breaking the constitutional link with the old country and forging independence for their new homeland.

Bitter experience of religious discrimination and economic deprivation were major factors for many of them after their movement from the north of Ireland to America through the 18th century from about 1717.

The Revolutionary War was fought over three fronts - along the eastern coastal states where the patriots came into direct conflict with the British army and naval forces; in the middle country of the Carolinas where rebels and loyalists fought it out and along the outer frontier where the settler militia units took on the Indian tribes who were on the side of the British.

On all three fronts, the Scots-Irish were in the vanguard of patriot involvement, but it was in the frontier lands that they made their most significant contribution. Quite uniquely, as a people they rose to the awesome challenge of the American frontier - its danger; its impenetrability and sheer enormity.

At the outbreak of the Revolutionary War in 1775, up to 20 per cent of the white population in the 13 American colonies was Scots and Scots-Irish, next to persons of English ancestry, and with such numbers the influence was considerable.

The challenge for the frontier settlers to provide their own protection came to a head in the French-Indian War of 1754-63. Until then, everything west of the Appalachian colonies was French and the French were using the Indians to keep the English and kindred settler groups on the eastern side of the mountains.

Pennsylvania was a main battlefield in the French-Indian War and it was there that the Scots-Irish made their initial appearance on American soil as a cohesive fighting unit. Of the 13 American colonies then, Pennsylvania was the least prepared for war, ruled as it was from Philadelphia by the pacifist Quakers and the Scots-Irish settlers on its frontiers were left particularly vulnerable to attack from the Indian tribes of the Shawnee and Delaware nations.

The Quakers had been in Pennsylvania since 1681 and by 1715 they represented the largest single element in the white population, administering the colonial system on behalf of the Crown. However, as the 18th century progressed and the tens of thousands of immigrants from the north of Ireland, England and Scotland arrived, Quaker control of affairs began to wane.

In 1766, Benjamin Franklin, the leading Philadelphia politician, estimated the population of Pennsylvania at 160,000, with about one-third of them Quakers. Others felt this was an exaggeration, stating the number of Quakers in 1775 at around 25,000. By this time, the Scots-Irish and German settlements could each muster higher proportions of the population.

Indian attacks on the Scots-Irish settlements had reached a climax in September and October, 1755, with the log cabins burned and many of the settlers either massacred or captured and held for torture. As lives were taken, and the Scots-Irish settlers forced to flee from their frontier outposts, the placid Quaker assembly in Philadelphia ignored the danger, with somewhat indifference and a large degree of incompetence.

The Quaker assembly recoiled in horror at the prospect of declaring war against the French-backed Indians as Scots-Irish anger at the ineptitude of their political masters rose to boiling point. Finally, realising the danger, Pennsylvania Governor Robert Hunter Morris seized the initiative and proclaimed war against the Shawnees and the Delawares, offering bounties for their scalps.

The Quakers were aghast at the measures, but they soon found that the wider Pennsylvania populace would no longer tolerate their neglect in providing defence for the colony.

The struggle between the Quakers and the Scots-Irish had also intensified through Quaker attempts to change Pennsylvania from a proprietary to a royal colony. The Quakers wanted Pennsylvania to be placed under the authority of a King who was "justly celebrated for his tender regard to the constitutional rights of Englishmen". The Scots-Irish were appalled, they held George III in no such esteem.

Quaker politicians in Philadelphia were inclined to frown disdainfully on the Scots-Irish, with leading theorist John Dickinson proclaiming they were "strangers to our laws and customs".

By 1756, however the Quakers were beginning to effectively lose control of Pennsylvania - power they were never to regain again in America after it fell completely from their grasp in the 1770s. American historian Wayland Dunaway said the fundamental issue between the Scots-Irish and the Quakers was whether Pennsylvania should be a democracy or an oligarchy.

Inevitably, steps were taken to properly arm the Pennsylvania province for an engagement that was to evolve over a decade and a half to the Revolutionary War.

Two hundred forts were erected on the frontier with money raised to buy arms. The Scots-Irish settlements of farmers, craftsmen and traders had now stretched extensively from Philadelphia down the south east of the province through Chester, York, Lancaster and Bucks counties and were heading west towards Fort Pitt (Pittsburgh). They were an increasingly vocal lobby for change!

They organised voluntary bands of frontiersmen, known as rangers, to defend their homes against the Indians and they provided the manpower for the militia units. At this precise point in American history, the Scots-Irish set down a marker that when it came to attacks on their hearth and home, and in the engagements of war, they were a people not to be trifled with.

Isaac Sharples, the noted Quaker scholar and historian, paid tribute to the contribution of the Scots-Irish in the ranks of the Pennsylvania Line, referred to by General Henry Lee as "The Line of Ireland." Sharples wrote: "The Scotch-Irishman did not waver, he now had the chance for which he was waiting. The Revolution was at least three-fourths a Presbyterian (Scotch-Irish) movement."

Throughout the colonies generally the Scots-Irish rallied strongly to the patriot cause, especially in Pennsylvania, Virginia and the Carolinas. In Pennsylvania they provided more officers and soldiers than any other racial strain.

The Scots-Irish, numbering about a quarter of the Pennsylvania population, suffered severely during the French-Indian War, but it was they who provided the leadership and the backbone of the successful resistance in the fierce conflict.

The Scots-Irish battles with the Indian tribes in the years leading up to, during and after the Revolutionary War were quite decisive in creating the American nation. Indeed, the major events from 1755 to 1790 centred around the Appalachian territory and the gaps in them where the frontier settlers had to enter to progress towards the new lands.

The Mohawk was the largest of the Appalachian gaps, and the only one essentially at sea level. The gap that linked Philadelphia and Pittsburgh in Pennsylvania was very high and not as easily accessible in the early years of settlement, while the Cumberland Gap was the main entry to the Kentucky and Tennessee lands and beyond the Ohio River towards the Mississippi.

There was also a fourth passage of movement for the settlers, around the Appalachian mountains by going south via Georgia and

Alabama. Of course, the frontier settlers were forbidden in a decree from King George 111 (the Proclamation Line of 1763) to go across the mountain, but there was a common and very apt saying by the stubborn Scots-Irish at the time - "It's a long way to London".

The first chink of defiance to the King's edict came in 1772 at Watauga in a part of North Carolina of what today is part of the state of Tennessee. After leasing two large tracts of land from the Cherokees, the settlers were not for moving and eventually they managed to purchase the land deeds from the Indians.

The Wataugans (the first batch were 16 families from North Carolina, mostly Scots-Irish led by Colonel John Sevier and Colonel James Robertson) moved on to lands that were officially designated Cherokee country, much to the consternation of Lord Dunmore, the royal governor of Virginia. An incensed Dunmore reported back to London that there were "a set of people in the back country of the colony, bordering on Cherokee country, who, finding they could not obtain the land they fancied here, have set up a separate state".

Under the colonial laws of King George 111, the Wataugans were squatters on Indians lands, but finding possession nine-tenths of the law they steadfastly stood their ground and ignored all the enforcements from Dunmore and the other colonial leaders.

The Wataugans set up their own militia and entered into negotiations with the Indians, first to lease the lands from the Cherokees and then to make a permanent purchase. They were 100 years later described by President Theodore Roosevelt as "a people who bid defiance to outsiders".

The Watauga Presbyterian settlers used the theology of manifest destiny to define their attitudes to far-off London rule, maintaining: "If God did not want us to have this land, we would not be out here". As was the case in Ulster during the 17th century Scottish Plantation there, so it was in the 18th century settlements of the Appalachian backcountry, as God had intended.

This was meant to be, and. with such a mindset, the Scots-Irish found the courage, determination and feeling that they were doing God's will in settling along the American frontier and pushing civilisation to the outer limits.

Of course, the official response to Scots-Irish demands for frontier land was documented in the 1720s by Ulster-born Quaker James Logan, the Provincial Secretary of Pennsylvania, who declared: "The Scotch-Irish maintain that it is against the laws of God and nature, that so much land should be idle, while so many Christians wanted it to labor on and to raise their bread."

Professor George Schweitzer, of the University of Tennessee in Knoxville, attributes, almost exclusively to the Scots-Irish, the American frontier action against British colonial interests for 40 years up to 1790.

"They were the frontiersmen; they did it, they penetrated the Appalachians; they fought the Revolution on the frontier. It is important to realise the immigrant settlers, particularly the Scots-Irish, did not bring all of their problems with them from the homelands.

"A great deal of it was engendered by the environment in which they were put. The Scots-Irish obviously left Ulster with many grievances, but their actions were quickened by their experiences on the ground when they arrived in America and tasted freedom, far removed from the diktats of monarchy and established church. They seized the opportunity and their whole social scene and outlook changed in the clamour for independence," said Professor Schweitzer.

In context, it was observed that the Scots-Irish were long accustomed, from both ancient memories and from their recent experiences in the north of Ireland, to an attitude of hostility towards the English, and, being a politically-minded people, they were highly sensitive to any wrongs or fancied wrongs inflicted upon them by the government in London, or by colonial governors in America carrying out its instructions.

The separation of church from state was fundamental to the thinking of Scots-Irish Presbyterians in America. One of their leaders during the Revolutionary War period - Scottish-born the Rev John Witherspoon, the only clergyman among the 56 signatories of the Declaration of Independence - justified opposition to the link-up between church and state with the words - "God alone is the Lord of the conscience".

Witherspoon, who, before he moved from Scotland to America had been involved in the revolt against the established Anglican

Church, was a prolific pamphleteer and in his sermons he used every opportunity to advocate a disengagement of church from state.

The terminology of Witherspoon was clear and unequivocal: "No compulsion ought to be used to constrain men's choice in the matter of religion" and "Has not every man a natural right, to judge for himself in matters of religion?"

He promised students at his College of New Jersey that "every denomination may have free and equal advantages of education . . . any different sentiments in religion notwithstanding."

The Witherspoon theory can be summarised in three clauses: that God alone is Lord of the conscience; that freedom of conscience is an inalienable right and that the state has no authority either to grant or deny religious liberty

Historian J. A. Froude very accurately summed up the situation of the Scots-Irish Presbyterians at the time of the Revolutionary War, thus: "The resentment which they carried with them continued to burn in their new home, and in the War of Independence England had no fiercer enemies than the grandsons and great grandsons of the Presbyterians who held Ulster for the Crown."

Colonel A. K. McClure, the distinguished Philadelphia writer, went even further: "It was the Scotch-Irish people of the colonies that made the Declaration of 1776. Without them it would not have been thought of except as a fancy. The actions of the Continental Congress voiced the teachings of the Scotch-Irish people of the land.

"They did not falter, they did not dissemble, they did not temporise. It was not the Quaker, not the Puritan, not the Cavalier; not even the Huguenot or the German; it was the Scotch-Irish of the land whose voice was first heard in Virginia.

"In the valley of Virginia, in North Carolina, in Cumberland and Westmoreland counties of Pennsylvania, the Scotch-Irish had declared that these colonies are, and of right, ought to be free and independent. They had taught this not only in their public speeches, but at their altars, in their pulpits, at their firesides, and it was from these that came that outburst of rugged and determined people that made the Declaration of 1776 possible.

"They were its authors, and they were ready to maintain it by all the moral and physical power they possessed. They meant that Scotch-

Irish blood was ready to flow on the battlefield, and come weal or woe, they would maintain it with their lives."

The 1776 Pennsylvania Constitution, which had as its cornerstone the Declaration of Independence, is looked upon as the "high-water mark" of radicalism during the American Revolution. It was the product of the victory by backcountry Scots-Irish farmers and Philadelphia artisans over the Quaker ruling class.

Historian John C. Miller recounts that it was majority rule in Pennsylvania under the constitution of 1776 and the privileged Quaker class was stripped of its power as the centre of gravity shifted from "the polite and genteel citizens of Philadelphia to the rough Scots-Irish farmers of the west and the plebeians of the metropolis".

"It is a fact that the Irish immigrants and their children are now in possession of the government of Pennsylvania, by their majority in the Assembly, as well as a great part of the territory; and I remember the first ship that brought them over," wrote Benjamin Franklin in 1784.

The very substantial role which the Scots-Irish played in heralding in the new American nation is not as widely known in modern-day United States society as it should.

There were two great waves of emigration from Ireland to America - the Presbyterian exodus from Ulster in the 18th century and the Roman Catholic movement from the southern counties after the great Irish famine of the 1840s. As first Americans on the frontier, the Scots-Irish were in at the start and moulded society.

As visionary leaders and brave foot soldiers of the Revolution, the Scots-Irish moved on to patiently fashion with others of like mind a political dynasty and confederation of states that was to evolve in the space of 200 years as the most prosperous and powerful nation in the world.

In the making and shaping of the United States of America, and in perpetuating the union of states from the Atlantic coastline to the Pacific, the efforts of the Scots-Irish were certainly considerable and meaningful!

2

Historical perceptions of the Scots-Irish
Revolutionary War influence

Reputable historians over the past two centuries are agreed that Scots-Irish support for American independence was generally ardent. The commitment to the patriot cause by the immigrant families from Ulster manifested itself in the actual fighting in the Revolutionary War and their courage and devotion to duty was a shining example.

Scots-Irish backing in the 1770s for breaking the colonial link with Britain was practically unanimous in Pennsylvania, Virginia, New Jersey and Massachusetts and in large settlements in North Carolina, South Carolina and Georgia similar sentiments were expressed and acted upon with fervour.

Many Scots-Irish families, however, in the South Carolina Piedmont area remained loyal to the Crown, and fought bitter battles against American patriots from the same ethnic community. But, at least three-quarters of the Scots-Irish backed the struggle for independence.

They played a key role in ushering in the new American nation, at both the level of leadership in politics and in the armed forces, and as foot soldiers of the Revolution. In the making of America, the Scots-Irish were most certainly in the vanguard and their contribution was monumental.

The Scots-Irish in the Shenandoah Valley of Virginia were particularly patriotic. The people of Augusta county, which had a predominance of Scots-Irish settlers, sent 137 barrels of flour to relieve the poor of Boston after the Boston "Tea Party" in 1773.

The main town in Rockbridge county, another Scots-Irish strong-hold, was named Lexington after the opening battle of the War in Massachusetts in 1775. And the classical academy in Lexington, founded by Ulster Presbyterian clergy, changed its name to Liberty Hall (later becoming in 1798 the Washington and Lee University!) and resolutions in support of American independence by staff and students were frequent.

The French-Indian War of 1754-63 proved to be an effective train-ing ground for the revolutionary forces in America, particularly those from the Scots-Irish settlements, and, in this earlier conflict, the armies in the Lake George and Lake Champlain region (Fort Henry, Ticonderoga and other frontier posts) and Montreal were largely made up of men of Scottish and Ulster-Scottish origin who inhabited the highly dangerous territory.

In Pennsylvania, in Kittanning and Fort Duquesne, the American forces fighting the French and the Indians were almost exclusively Ulster-Scots, who were largely responsible for the reversal of General Edward Braddock's defeat. They were the people who erected the forts and organised local militia, called Rifle Rangers, frontline units which were eventually incorporated into George Washington's army.

The Scots-Irish have always been a patriotic people, with a strong fighting tradition. On the American frontier in the 18th century, one had to possess these sturdy qualities to defend family, home and property and, more than any other race, the Scots-Irish stood out.

They were successful, through their exploits in the French-Indian and Revolutionary Wars, in opening the way for the advancing settlements of western Pennsylvania and the Ohio Valley, down to the Mississippi and beyond..

William C. Lehmann, in his book Scottish-Irish Contributions to Early American Life and Culture, interestingly observes that the brunt of the fighting in Pennsylvania fell to the Scots-Irish by default. "The Quakers were pacifist and the Germans lacked a tradition of political involvement and generally lived in the more settled regions," he said.

T. J. Werterbaker (author of Early Scotch Contributions to the United States - published Glasgow, 1945), praising the excellence of the American soldiers who were Scots-Irish, said they were "the back-bone" of George Washington's army, with the famous Pennsylvania

Line mostly of this vintage. "At Valley Forge when many deserted him, they remained, despite cold and hunger, to keep alive the waning cause."

George Washington, of course, said: "If defeated everywhere else, I will make my stand for liberty among the Scots-Irish in my native Virginia."

The town of New Londonderry in New Hampshire - first settled in the early 1720s by Ulster Presbyterians from the Bann Valley around Coleraine and Ballymoney - sent more soldiers to aid George Washington's armies than any other colonial town.

Ralph Barton Perry (author of Puritanism and Democracy - published New York 1944) said that "when account is taken of the Scotch-Irish Presbyterians, the Germans of the middle and southern colonies and the New England congregationalists, it is safe to say that the bulk of the revolutionary armies came from dissenters of the Reformed or Calvinistic sects. From the clergy of these sects came also the religious leadership."

A citation submitted by a British major-general to a House of Commons committee in London stated that "half the Continental Army were from Ireland" - Scots-Irish.

General Nathaniel Greene, one of George Washington's Continental Army commanders and who gave Lord Charles Cornwallis a "bloody nose" at the battle of Guilford Courthouse in March, 1781, thought highly of the mostly Scots-Irish settlers who had just moved down the Great Wagon Road into the Carolina backcountry.

"Coastal dwellers are sickly, but indifferent militia, but the backcountry people are bold and daring in their make-up," he said.

The British Government of the day, of course, was well aware of the Scots-Irish leanings in the war, thus the remark by Prime Minister Horace Walpole, who said in a jibe to his cabinet: "I hear that our American cousin has run off with a Presbyterian parson".

This view was shared by Captain Johann Heinrchs, of the Hessian Jaeger Corps in British service: "Call it not an American rebellion, it is nothing more nor less than an Irish-Scotch Presbyterian rebellion."

A representative of Lord Dartmouth, writing from New York in November, 1776, agreed: "Presbyterianism is really at the bottom of this whole conspiracy, has supplied it with vigour, and will never rest until something is decided upon."

Jonathan D. Sergeant, member of the Continental Congress from New Jersey, said that the Scots-Irish were the main pillar supporting the Revolution in Pennsylvania.

Horace Walpole and others in the court of King George 111 in London were convinced the whole war was nothing more than an uprising of rabble-rousing Presbyterians, largely Scots-Irish - "a sort of latter-day Cromwellian outburst against the due civil, ecclesiastical and political order of a sensible and free British Empire".

It was significant that the only churchman in the American Continental Congress of 1776 was Scottish-born Presbyterian cleric the Rev John Witherspoon and he was a principal signatory of the Declaration.

Daniel I. Rupp (author of History and Topography of Pennsylvania counties - Lancaster, Pennsylvania 1846) stated: "When the alarm of the American Revolution echoed along the rocky walls of the Blue Mountains, it awakened a congenial thrill of blood of that race which years before, in Ireland and Scotland, has resisted the arbitrary powers of England."

David Ramsey, son of Ulster emigrants and considered the "most remarkably judicious" of early historians of the American Revolution, noted: "The Irish in America, with a few exceptions, were attached to independence, Presbyterians and therefore mostly Whigs. They are inferior to none in discipline, courage or attachment to the cause."

General William Howe, a British commander in the War, spoke of the excellent markmanship of the Scots-Irish - "learned as hunters and Indian fighters, and to their rifles perfected with knowledge of ballistics". Another British officer referred to patriot forces in Pennsylvania during the War as the "line of Ireland".

Tennessee state historian and author Wilma Dykeman observed that the Scots-Irish character - "prompt to resent an affront, unrelenting to foes" - was to leave an imprint on the history of the Revolutionary War at Kings Mountain.

"The Scotch-Irish were the group that left their image stamped indelibly on the frontier. They were both venturesome and cautious, taciturn to a fault, but spoke their mind freely when aroused. Friend and foe alike were objects of their steadfast attention and their nature rebelled against anything that savoured of injustice or deceit, nor did they take kindly to restraint of any kind," she said.

Dr Thomas Smyth, in his critique, said: "The battles of Cowpens and Kings Mountain are amongst the most celebrated as giving a turning point to the contests of the Revolutionary War. General Daniel Morgan, who commanded the patriots at Cowpens on January 17, 1781, was a Presbyterian elder and lived and died in the communion of that Church.

"General Andrew Pickens, who made all the arrangements for the battle of Cowpens, was also a Presbyterian elder of Ulster stock from the South Carolina Piedmont and nearly all under his command were Presbyterians.

"In the earlier battle of Kings Mountain, on October 7, 1780, Colonel William Campbell, Colonel James Williams (who fell in action), Colonel Benjamin Cleveland, Colonel Isaac Shelby and Colonel John Sevier (of Huguenot stock) were all Presbyterian elders and the body of troops were collected from the Presbyterian settlements."

The Scots-Irish, of course, had made a significant contribution in the first years of the War, with their hardy and skilled marksmen taking a leading part in the defeat, surrender and capture of British soldiers under General John Burgoyne at the battles of Saratoga along the Hudson River in September-October, 1777.

American historian George Bancroft said the Scots-Irish brought to America no submissive love for England: and their experience and their religion alike bade them meet opposition with prompt resistance.

"The first voice publicly raised in America to dissolve all connection with Great Britain came not from the Puritans of New England or the Dutch of New York or the planters of Virginia, but the Scots-Irish," Bancroft pointed out.

"The Presbyterians of Pennsylvania and throughout the colonies arose as one man for the rights and liberties of America," he added.

Another distinguished 19th century historian J. A. Froude wrote: "Throughout the revolted colonies all evidence shows that the foremost, the most irreconcilable, the most determined in pushing the quarrel to the last extremity were the Scotch-Irish, whom the bishops, Lord Donegall and others of their kind, had driven out of Ulster."

Author W. F. T. Butler commented: "It was the Presbyterians of Ulster, driven from their homes by the mistaken religious and economic legislation of the 18th century, who furnished the backbone of the armies that put an end to the rule of England in what is now the United States".

President William McKinley, whose great-grandfather James emigrated from Co Antrim in 1743, said the Scots-Irish would not change either their ancestry or birthplace if they could.

"They are proud of both, but they are prouder yet of their new home they have helped create under the Stars and Stripes, the best and freest under the sun. The Scotch-Irish were not only well born, but they have improved upon their beginning, have progressed with their opportunities and have made opportunities when none seemed present.

"While he is distinctive as a type, a Scotch-Irishman is a racial evolution - the result of a slow fusion of diverse characteristics. Their deeds on behalf of American independence should ever be cherished in patriotic remembrance, and it is a remarkable fact - as observed by those who have taken the trouble to examine the matter - that it is only within the past years that recorded history has given just credit to the sturdy race, to whom George Washington looked as his never-failing support and as his forlorn hope when all others should have left him, when defeat should have encompassed him," said President McKinley.

"Representatives of the Scotch-Irish are among the brightest names in American history. They have shone in every great epoch of national life. So long as there is a struggle for human liberty, so long as patriotism has a place in the American heart, that long will the name and fame of our ancestors be preserved and enshrined," he added.

The Scots-Irish deserve an honoured place in the history of America. They were in it from the start and laid the foundations for freedom and democracy!

3

Scots-Irish signers of the
American Declaration of Independence

The 56 men from the thirteen colonies who signed the American Declaration of Independence in July, 1776 were almost entirely of British family origin. Thirty eight are firmly established as being of English extraction, eight Irish (including six Ulster-Scots), five Welsh, four pure Scottish and one Swedish.

Those with Ulster links were John Hancock, Thomas McKean, George Taylor, James Smith, Matthew Thornton and Edward Rutledge, with Thomas Lynch Jun and George Read from family ties to the south of Ireland. William Whipple, Robert Paine and Thomas Nelson are also believed to have links with the north of Ireland.

Of the 56 signatories of the Declaration, 24 were lawyers and jurists, eleven were merchants, nine farmers and the rest large plantation owners, men of means and well-educated.

PENNSYLVANIA (9) - Benjamin Franklin, Robert Morris, Benjamin Rush, John Morton, George Clymer, James Smith, George Taylor, James Wilson, George Ross.

VIRGINIA (7) - Thomas Jefferson, Richard Henry Lee, Benjamin Harrison, Francis Lightfoot Lee, Thomas Nelson, George Wythe, Carter Braxton.

MASSACHUSETTS (5) - Samuel Adams, John Hancock, John Adams, Elbridge Gerry, Robert Treat Paine.

NEW JERSEY (5) - John Witherspoon, Richard Stockton, Francis Hopkinson, John Hart, Abraham Clark.

CONNECTICUT (4) - Robert Sherman, Samuel Huntington, William Williams, Oliver Wolcott.

MARYLAND (4) - Charles Carroll, Thomas Stone, William Paca, Samuel Chase.

NEW YORK (4) - Philip Livingston, Lewis Morris, William Floyd, Francis Lewis.

SOUTH CAROLINA (4) - Thomas Heyward Jun., Arthur Middleton, Edward Rutledge, Thomas Lynch Jun.

DELAWARE (3) - Caesar Rodney, Thomas McKean, George Read.

GEORGIA (3) Lyman Hall, Button Guinnett, George Walton.

NEW HAMPSHIRE (3) - Josiah Bartlett, William Whipple, Matthew Thornton.

NORTH CAROLINA (3) - William Hooper, Joseph Hewes, John Penn.

RHODE ISLAND (2) - Stephen Hopkins, William Ellery.

* Ulster-born **Charles Thomson**, secretary to the American Continental Congress, also signed the Declaration, but strictly on account of the office that he held.

4

Thomas McKean - *leading advocate for Independence*

Thomas McKean, the leading Delaware signer of the Declaration of Independence, was the son of an Ulster emigrant from North Antrim who came to Pennsylvania via Londonderry as a child and later married into a well-connected and wealthy Scots-Irish family.

The McKeans of Co Antrim and Londonderry were descended from William McKean, who moved from Argyllshire in Scotland to Ulster in 1674 at the height of the Scottish Plantation.

The signer's father William became a tavern keeper in the Scots-Irish Presbyterian settlement stronghold of Chester county, Pennsylvania and he married Letitia Finney, whose family had also emigrated from the north of Ireland.

Their second son was Thomas and, along with his brother, he was educated by Donegal-born Presbyterian minister the Rev Francis Allison at his classical academy at New London, Pennsylvania. Continental Congress secretary Charles Thomson was also tutored by Dr Allison, formerly of Leck near Letterkenny.

Thomas McKean moved into law and he built up a flourishing practice in Pennsylvania and in the neighbouring states of Delaware and New Jersey. In Delaware he became attorney-general in 1756, clerk of the legislative assembly in 1757-59 and assembly member in 1762-79.

McKean married Mary Borden, eldest daughter of Colonel Joseph Borden, of New Jersey, and his connection with this prominent and wealthy family considerably widened his political horizon and influence. The marriage lasted 10 years, with Mary dying on the birth of her sixth child, and within 18 months Thomas had a second wife, Sarah Armitage, from New Castle, Delaware.

The couple moved to Pennsylvania in 1774 just as Revolutionary War clouds were gathering and, with McKean being noted for his outspoken comments against British rule in the colonies and opposition to the Stamp Act of 1765, he was an obvious champion of the patriot cause with the Philadelphia ruling classes.

McKean had led the movement in Delaware for the establishment of a colonial congress and he was a delegate from the colony at the first Continental Congress at Philadelphia in September, 1774. He served on 30 Congress committees and was strongly in favour of delegate Richard Henry Lee's resolution for independence.

However, a Delaware colleague George Read, who also favoured independence, was absent on militia duty when the crucial vote was being pushed through and, with the third delegate Caesar Rodney against breaking the ties with Britain and intending to cancel out McKean's vote, it created a dilemma. This resulted in McKean sending an envoy, at his own personal expense, to have Rodney ordered back to Philadelphia to vote.

Although he was a Delaware resident, McKean had also put his name among the persons residing in Philadelphia who were "able and willing to bear arms". When the independence vote was passed, McKean headed off immediately to Perth Amboy, New Jersey in command of a group of Pennsylvania "Associators" in support of George Washington's hard-pressed troops. This was the reason he was unable to sign the Declaration when it was engrossed and ready for signatures in early August.

After the War, McKean, under pressure from rivals challenging his legitimacy as a full-blooded assentor to the Declaration of Independence, explained his action in a letter to John Adams, later to become the second American President.

"After the 4th July, I was not in Congress for several months, having marched with a regiment of associators as colonel to support General Washington. When the associators were discharged, I returned to Philadelphia, took my seat in Congress and signed my name to the Declaration on parchment," he said.

It is believed McKean made the signing in January, 1777.

Thomas McKean became chief justice in Pennsylvania in 1777, a position he held for 22 years, and, as a Delaware representative, he was elected President of the Continental Congress in 1781, but only served for a few months. The holding of office in two states and his high profile involvement in the War created animosity for McKean.

At Christmas, 1780, he wrote a letter to the Delaware legislature, stating that both his health and fortune were impaired by his constant attention to public business and asking to be excused from attending congress. He was kept on, however, against his will, until the peace deal was signed in 1783.

The War and the political machinations had worn McKean out and in a letter to John Adams he told how he was "hunted like a fox by the enemy" and "compelled to remove my family five times in a few months, at last fixing them in a little log-house on the banks of the Susquehanna River, and they were soon obliged to move on account of the incursions of the Indians."

When the war ended, Thomas McKean, as a federalist, worked to ratify the Federal Constitution in the Pennsylvania convention of 1787. As he got older, it was observed that he had become less liberal in his views and some of his more conservative decisions as chief justice brought him into conflict with the Assembly and the military authorities.

He also moved away from federalism in the American administration due to the hostile foreign policy being adopted with France in the 1790s and in 1799 he was elected Governor of Pennsylvania as a Jeffersonian candidate. McKean was friendly disposed to the French, and remained antagonistic to Britain. He warmly embraced Thomas Jefferson's election as President in 1800.

To some, McKean was looked upon as a harsh, domineering man, but in a tribute, John Adams, the Massachusetts signer of the Declaration, said: "He appeared to me to see more clearly to the end of the business than any others of the whole body." Another description of him was that he was "cold in manner, energetic, independent, proud and vain, but with ability, candour and honesty."

McKean outlived almost all of the Declaration signers, dying in 1817, aged 83. Many of the signers lost everything they had during the

War, some were imprisoned and some went into bad health. McKean somehow managed to retain possession of large tracts of Pennsylvania land. History records him as one of the most influential of the Declaration signers.

The Ulsterman was there

Hi! Uncle Sam!
When freedom was denied you,
And Imperial might defied you,
Who was it stood beside you,
At Quabec and Brandywine?
And dared retreats and dangers
Redcoats and Hessian strangers
In the lean, long-rifled Rangers,
And the Pennsylvania Line!

Hi! Uncle Sam!
Wherever there was fighting,
Or wrong that needed righting,
An Ulsterman was sighting,
His Kentucky gun with care:
All the road to Yorktown,
From Lexington to Yorktown,
From Valley Forge to Yorktown
That Ulsterman was there!

Hi! Uncle Sam!
Virginia sent her brave men,
The North paraded grave men,
That they might not be slave men,
But ponder this with calm:
The first to face the Tory
And the first to lift Old Glory,
Made your War an Ulster story,
Think it over, Uncle Sam!

W. F. MARSHALL (REV),
Co Tyrone.

5

George Read - *the "honest lawyer" from Delaware*

George Read, Delaware signer of the American Declaration, was the son of a Dublin man John Read whose family were English aristocrats from Berkshire and who, when he arrived in Maryland from Ireland, married the daughter of a Welsh planter, Mary Howell.

The family moved to New Castle, Delaware and George grew up on a farm that overlooked the Delaware river. He was educated with the sons of Scots-Irish families in Chester, Pennsylvania and later at the classics academy in New London, run by Presbyterian minister the Francis Allison, from Letterkenny in Co Donegal.

Francis Allison also tutored Thomas McKean, another Delaware signer; Charles Thomson, secretary of the Continental Congress, and James Smith, a Declaration signer for Pennsylvania.

Read was admitted to the Philadelphia bar when only 20 and he returned to New Castle, Delaware to become widely known as the "honest lawyer". He married a widow, Mrs Gertrude Ross Till, sister of Scottish-born George Ross, the Pennsylvania signer, and in the same year was appointed attorney-general in Delaware.

When he first entered the Continental Congress in 1774, George Read was opposed to independence, but, having earlier campaigned against the introduction of the Stamp Act in 1766, he was considered to have some sympathies with the patriot cause.

His view on the Stamp Act was that "if this or any similar law imposing an internal tax for revenue was enforced", the colonists would fear they were about to become "slaves of Great Britain". To avoid that, they would resist.

As for the resolution for independence which came before Congress, Read thought it premature and refused to vote for it. However, once it was adopted by an overwhelming majority, he at once fell into line and "zealously upheld it", later supporting the new republic at the risk of his life.

When British forces captured Wilmington in September 1777 and captured Delaware's Ulster-born Governor John McKinly, Read assumed the Governor's duties. Hurrying back from Philadelphia by a roundabout route, Read and his family were halted by British forces, but explaining he was a country gentleman returning home he was allowed to pass through.

As Delaware Governor, Read raised troops, clothing and provisions for the Continental Army and he spread a new spirit of enthusiasm through a hitherto largely uncommitted state for the patriot cause.

Read went on to become a judge in the American court of appeals and he was one of his state's first United States senators. He was chief justice of Delaware when he died in 1798.

Thomas Read, George's younger brother, was an American naval officer who was master of vessels in the West Indies and Atlantic trade routes prior to being commissioned captain of the Pennsylvania navy in October, 1775, just as hostilities were commencing.

James Read, another brother, was a militia officer in Pennsylvania and a naval commissioner. He was recognised for gallant service at the battles of Trenton, Princeton, Brandywine and Germantown.

William Read, a third brother, was a merchant in Havana. Their father, John, was largely responsible for establishing Charleston in South Carolina as a main trade port in the American colonies

6

George Taylor - *moderate radical from the backcountry*

Declaration of Independence signer George Taylor emigrated from Ulster to Pennsylvania as a 20-year-old in the 1730s and he settled in the Scots-Irish dominated Chester county. Taylor was not a natural politician, having been thrust into the maelstrom of the patriot struggle centred on Philadelphia with support from the backcountry frontier settlers.

Taylor was in the iron producing business and his political career did not begin until he was a man in his mid-forties. He would have been classified as a moderate radical, who would have had more of a provincial outlook than the broader, far-reaching manifesto of the Philadelphia merchant and academic class.

With limited education, George Taylor's political ambitions did not extend beyond representing the small farmer settlers of south east Pennsylvania, but he nevertheless gets an honoured place in American history as one of the 56 signers of the July 4 1776 Declaration.

Taylor, elected to the provincial assembly at Philadelphia in 1764, was opposed to British Government rule in the colonies and, when the Stamp Act on direct taxation was passed at Westminster, he helped draw up a response from the Pennsylvania delegates to the Stamp Act Congress.

In July, 1775, Taylor was appointed colonel of the Bucks county militia and, although he never saw active service, he retained the title for the duration of the War.

After his August 2 signing, George Taylor was appointed a delegate to the second Continental Congress, replacing one of several Pennsylvanians who had refused to sign the Declaration. But he had little or no role in Congress business, other than to represent it at a conference with the Susquehanna Indians in 1777.

Taylor was elected to the Supreme Council of Pennsylvania, but served only six weeks because of illness. He died in 1781, aged 65.

The Ulster background of George Taylor is claimed to be based in Co. Antrim and some reports state that he was the son of a Presbyterian minister.

American Presidential Seal

7

James Smith - *popular man of the Pennsylvanian frontier*

James Smith, one of the lesser known signers of the American Declaration of Independence, was born in the north of Ireland about 1719 and arrived in Pennsylvania as a 10-year-old with his Presbyterian family, settling at Chester county in the south east of the colony.

John Smith, whose brothers had moved from Ulster to America before him, became a successful farmer and son James was taught at the classics academy of Co. Donegal-born cleric the Rev Francis Allison, where other Scots-Irish principals of the Revolutionary struggle were educated.

James Smith emerged as a lawyer, supplementing his income as a land surveyor, and as the colonists' dissatisfaction grew over the arbitrary rule from London he became a leader of the popular feeling in Chester county.

In 1774, Smith submitted a paper on the constitutional power of Great Britain over the colonies in America, in which he urged an end to the import of British goods and promoted the idea of a general congress of the 13 colonies, where colonial grievances and ambitions could be discussed and shared. The idea spawned the Continental Congress he was to become a member of.

Smith went on raise a volunteer militia group in York, Pennsylvania and was appointed captain. This company grew into a battalion ready for action in the War, with Smith rising to the honorary title of colonel. He was a delegate to the provincial convention in Philadelphia in January, 1775 and in July of that year was elected to the Continental Congress. He signed the Declaration of Independence soon after July 4, 1776.

When Congress met in York, Pennsylvania, meetings of the board of war were held in Smith's law office. On retirement from Congress, Smith was a judge in the Pennsylvania High Court of Errors and Appeals and in 1782 he became brigadier-general of the militia and counsellor for the Pennsylvania-Connecticut Wyoming Valley controversy.

During the last 20 years of his career this highly popular personality of the Pennsylvania frontier acquired a substantial land estate. He was a man possessed with a sharp wit, a lively somewhat eccentric manner and an exceptional memory. He was a public figure who made good company and attracted to himself many friends.

Smith's constituency was mainly the Scots-Irish settlements of the Pennsylvania backcountry and over several decades he faithfully championed their cause in Philadelphia.

Tragically, all of James Smith's official papers from his highly significant involvement in the Revolutionary War period were destroyed in a fire at his office a year before he died in 1806, aged 85. He is buried in the cemetery of the English Presbyterian Church in Pennsylvania.

"I love Highlanders, but when I come to the branch that has been grafted on to the Ulster stem I take off my hat in veneration and awe!"

LORD ROSEBERRY.

8

Matthew Thornton - *a doctor who resisted tyranny*

Religious persecution forced the Presbyterian Thornton family to migrate through four countries in about 100 years, and the trauma was to leave its mark on descendants, most notable among them Matthew Thornton, one of the signers of the American Declaration of Independence in 1776.

The Thorntons were of English origin and their religious convictions to the Calvinist faith forced them to move to Scotland, from where, during the unsettled reign of Charles 1 of the mid-17th century, they transplanted to a new life in Londonderry county in the north of Ireland.

Life was just as difficult for the several generations of the Thorntons in Ulster and, on August 4, 1718, James Thornton and his family were among 120 families who landed at Boston in five ships, after leaving their Lower Bann homeland centred on the towns of Coleraine and Ballymoney.

The four-year-old Thornton son Matthew never forgot his first impressions of American frontier life even for one so young, particularly in that uncomfortable first winter housed on board the cramped ship that had brought them across the Atlantic.

From the ship they transferred to the township of Worcester in Massachusetts, where Matthew went to school, studying medicine. Worcester was an English Puritan town where intolerance of the Ulster Presbyterians manifested itself in a very pronounced way during the decade following their arrival in America.

In the mid-1730s, James Thornton and his Scots-Irish kinsfolk were forced to move on to the neighbouring town of Pelham, but son Matthew, by this stage graduated as a doctor, decided to go further north and settle in the older and more thriving settlement of Londonderry, New Hampshire. There, he established a large and profitable medical practice.

In 1745, Dr Thornton accompanied the military expedition against the French Fort Louisburg on Cape Breton Island and on his return increased his extensive estate. He bought his father's 170 acres at Pelham and extended this with the purchase of an additional 150 acres.

He was elected in 1758 to represent Londonderry in the Provincial legislature and, still showing some sympathy for colonial rule, was commissioned as colonel of the Londonderry regiment of militia. However, his attitude to London had changed by the early 1770s, when, revolted by the effects of the Stamp Act, he joined the patriot activists clamouring for independence.

By 1775, Thornton was publicly denouncing the "unconstitutional and tyrannical acts of the British Parliament" and he was elected as president of the Fourth Provincial Congress. In early 1776, he helped draw up a plan for the government of New Hampshire to counter British rule and this became the constitution of the state, until 1783. It was the first written constitution of any of the American states.

Matthew Thornton signed the American Declaration of Independence on November 4, 1776 when he went to the Second Continental Congress in Philadelphia as a representative from New Hampshire. He was the last to sign that year and was one of the signers who had not been in Congress to hear the June resolution, nor the early July debates on the Declaration.

He served only part of a year in Congress and, although ill-health forced him to retire from public life, he managed to live until he was 89, dying at Newburyport, Massachussetts in 1803.

Matthew Thornton, an impressive looking man, dark and six feet tall with a plain and unassuming but droll personality, did not marry until he was 48. His wife Hannah Jack, of Chester, New Hampshire, also came from a Scots-Irish family, with Co. Tyrone roots.

9

Edward and John Rutledge - *declaring for independence in South Carolina*

The Rutledges of Co Tyrone are one of the best-known families who emigrated from Ulster in the 18th century. This is largely due to the contribution of Edward Rutledge, South Carolina governor and a signatory of the American Declaration of Independence, and his brother John, who was also a South Carolina governor.

Dr John Rutledge, Edward's father, left the north of Ireland in 1735 and, shortly after arrival in Charleston, he married 15-year-old Sarah Hext. The couple had seven children, with Edward, the youngest, just a year old when his father died.

The Rutledges were a well-connected affluent family and after Edward Rutledge got his early education in Charleston, he was sent to London to study law at the Temple Bar, where his eldest brother John had also been called. Five years later he returned to South Carolina and his public life began in July, 1774 when he was elected to the First Continental Congress in Philadelphia along with brother John.

The Rutledges talked and argued a lot in the Congress debates, much to the irritation of some in the chamber, but more senior colleagues like US President-to-be John Adams and Benjamin Franklin put this down to their youthful vigour and obvious commitment to the American patriot cause.

Edward Rutledge had made himself popular in Charleston by instituting legal proceedings on behalf of Thomas Robinson, publisher of the South Carolina Gazette, who had been imprisoned for printing his newspaper on unstamped paper, thereby violating the disputed Stamp Act, initiated from London.

The Rutledges were re-elected for a second Congressional term in February 1776 and, as John returned to South Carolina to canvas opinion on support for independence, his brother maintained a presence in the Philadelphia legislature.

When word came through from Charleston on July 2 that South Carolina was weighing in behind independence, Edward Rutledge and three other South Carolina delegates - Thomas Heyward Jun., Arthur Middleton and Thomas Lynch Jun. signed the Declaration. Rutledge was the second youngest signer.

In November of that year, Edward returned to take command of the Charleston battalion of artillery and as captain of that unit he was involved in a number of battles, including the defence of Charleston. When the city fell to the British in May, 1780, Rutledge was captured and sent to St Augustine, Florida, but in July, 1781, along with Thomas Heyward and Arthur Middleton, he was involved in prisoner exchange and set free.

Rutledge was soon back in his state legislature and he drew up the bill proposing the confiscation of the properties of all Crown loyalists, feeling this measure was necessary to negate the pro-British sympathies which were still deeply embedded, particularly in parts of the South Carolina Piedmont area among elements of the Scots-Irish.

When the war ended, Rutledge, a rapid conservative, continued to represent South Carolina in Congress until 1796. He was also a US senator and in 1798 became governor of South Carolina, but his health at this time was poor and he died in January 1800, aged only 51. Edward Rutledge was married twice, to Henrietta Middleton, a sister of his fellow signer Arthur Middleton, and on her death 18 years later to widow Mary Shubrick Eveleigh.

John Rutledge was the first patriot Governor of South Carolina, elected in 1779, and he managed to escape the city just before it was captured by the British in May, 1780. He turned up in North Carolina and joined the army of General Horatio Gates and visited Philadelphia to lobby George Washington and the Continental Congress to send American regulars to liberate the South.

After the war, John Rutledge was elected chief justice of South Carolina and senior associate justice of the US Supreme Court. He also died in 1800, aged 61.

American historian R. L. Meriwether said of John Rutledge: "He was the most gifted and devoted leader of the ruling group of 18th century South Carolina. He embodied, perhaps, more perfectly than any other man, the ideas of his class".

Another of the Rutledge clan from Co Tyrone to distinguish himself in the Revolutionary War was George Rutledge, who was a militia officer at the Battle of Kings Mountain in October, 1780.

George (born in Co Tyrone in 1755) was brigadier general and state militia commander when John Sevier was appointed as first Tennessee governor in 1796 and he represented Sullivan county in the Tennessee legislature. His wife was Annie Armstrong, of a Co. Fermanagh family who had moved from the Shenandoah Valley of Virginia.

George Rutledge's family can be traced back to George and Nelly Gamble Rutledge from Co Tyrone, whose five children William, Thomas, John, Jane and Catherine emigrated with their off-spring to America in 1763, and they too moved through the Shenandoah Valley, settling at Tinkling Spring at Staunton, and worshipping at the Presbyterian Church there. George's father William married Eleanor Caldwell, from Co Cavan.

The grandfather of Thomas Lynch Jun., one of the four South Carolina representatives and the youngest at 26 to sign the Declaration of Independence, was also born in Ireland and settled as a wealthy estate-owner in the colonial territory around Charleston.

Thomas Lynch Jun., although born in Winyaw, South Carolina, was educated at Eton and Cambridge in England, and graduated in law at the Middle Temple in London. He was elected to the South Carolina Provincial Congress and in 1775 was appointed captain of the First South Carolina Regiment, before he and his father Thomas moved to the Continental Congress in Philadelphia.

Thomas Lynch Sen. took seriously ill early in 1776 and he died before the Declaration could be signed later that year. Thomas Jun., however, was on hand to vote for independence on behalf of his state and to sign the document in his father's absence. His health was also poor, largely as a result of a "swamp fever" or malaria he picked up while in war service in North Carolina. He died in 1779, aged only 30.

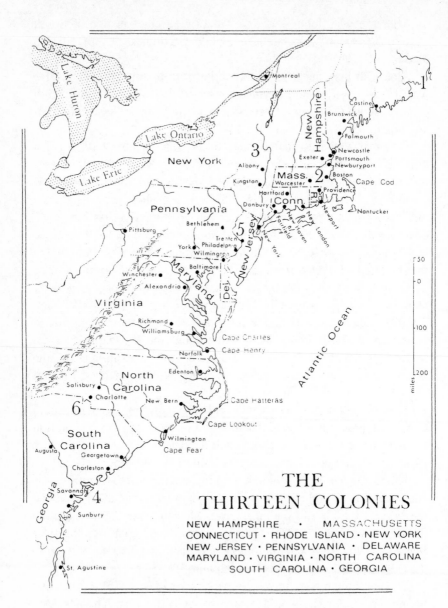

THE THIRTEEN COLONIES

NEW HAMPSHIRE · MASSACHUSETTS
CONNECTICUT · RHODE ISLAND · NEW YORK
NEW JERSEY · PENNSYLVANIA · DELAWARE
MARYLAND · VIRGINIA · NORTH CAROLINA
SOUTH CAROLINA · GEORGIA

1. Naval action in Machias Bay, June 12, 1775.   2. Seige of Boston, April 1775 – March 1776.   3. Battle of Saratoga, October 1777.   4. Seige of Savannah, September – October 1779.   5. Mutiny of the Pennsylvania Line, January 1781.   6. Battle of King's Mountain, October 1780.

The thirteen American Colonies

10

Rev. John Witherspoon - *only cleric to sign the Declaration*

Scotsman the Rev John Witherspoon was the only cleric, and arguably the best educated, to sign the Declaration of Independence and his influence with his Presbyterian kinsmen from Ulster in Pennsylvania was considerable.

Witherspoon, a son of the Presbyterian manse from Edinburgh, emigrated in 1768 with his wife Elizabeth Montgomery, from Craighouse, Ayrshire, to take up the post of principal at Princeton College in New Jersey, founded by Co Armagh man the Rev William Tennent.

At first, Witherspoon believed clergy should avoid becoming embroiled in political matters, but King George III and the London Parliament's handling of the American colonies caused him to stand alongside the patriot cause.

Though he initially shied away from controversial political ideas in his sermons, John Witherspoon wrote essays, arguments and opinions on these matters which enjoyed a large circulation. Back home in Scotland, he was labelled a rebel and a traitor.

Not all Presbyterians accepted Witherspoon's analysis on the concept of political independence from Britain, even considering the animosity between the Church of England (Episcopal) and Presbyterianism. Some conservatives, many of them upper-class merchants, feared for the economic and security consequences in a withdrawal from the British Empire.

Presbyterian radicals, consisting of "middle sort" frontier stock and working class urban folk, advanced the revolutionary ideals by substantiating claims of discriminatory British policies against their interests over many years and worked to undermine the influence of the ruling colonial classes.

John Witherspoon gathered around him a group of academics and lawyers and, gradually, they succeeded in wresting power from the Quakers, the power-brokers in Philadelphia since William Penn first settled the region at the start of the 18th century.

Witherspoon's closest allies in the radical campaign included Co Londonderry-born Charles Thomson, the Continental Congress secretary; John Livingston, a New York publisher, and the Rev Joseph Clark and the Rev James Armstrong, who were to become Moderators of the American Presbyterian General Assembly and militia officers.

Such was the Presbyterian Church influence in pursuing the patriot cause that in 1776 loyalist cleric the Rev Dr Charles Inglis, rector of Trinity Church in New York, remarked: "I do not know one Presbyterian minister, nor have I been able, after strict inquiry, to hear of any who did not by preaching and every effort in their power promote all the measures of the Continental Congress, however, extravagant."

John Witherspoon, in his broad Scottish burr, explained his commitment to constitutional change in a submission he made just before the signing of the Declaration in 1776: "There is not a single instance in history in which civil liberty was lost and religious liberty preserved entirely. If therefore we yield up our temporal property, we at the same time deliver the conscience into bondage," he said.

Witherspoon was chosen as the New Jersey delegate to the Continental Congress in June, 1776, serving until 1782, and when the resolution of independence was debated on July 1 and 2, he spoke strongly in favour of adopting it without delay.

The feisty Scot paid a heavy price for his radicalism and when British forces moved in on Princeton in November, 1776, the college was forced to close. Witherspoon had to flee for his life, as the Redcoats plundered the college and burned the fine library.

Within a month George Washington drove the British out at the battle of Princeton, but college work was not resumed until the following autumn.

Witherspoon died in 1794, aged 71, after years of declining health.

James Wilson, another Scot from Edinburgh who emigrated in 1765, was a Declaration signer for Pennsylvania and, as a lawyer, he practiced first with the German settlers (Pennsylvania Dutch) and then among the Scots-Irish in Carlisle.

He became an extensive farmer and land speculator and played a prominent part in the patriot struggle alongside Charles Thomson and Edward Rutledge.

Thomas Nelson, whose family came from Penrith on the Scottish borders and had Ulster connections, was a Continental Congress delegate from Virginia who carried to Philadelphia his state's resolution demanding separation from Britain.

Nelson was a very generous contributor to patriot funds during the Revolutionary War and, at the siege of Yorktown in 1781, he commanded the Virginia militia. He became governor of Virginia.

"Scotch Tom", Thomas Nelson's father, settled at Yorktown and became a wealthy merchant and landowner.

> *"All America lies at the end of the wilderness road, and our past is no dead past, but still lives on within us. Our forefathers had civilisation inside themselves, the wild outside. We live in the civilisation they created, but within us the wilderness still lingers. What they dreamed we live, and, what they lived, we dream"*
>
> T. K. WHIPPLE,
> Study Out The Land.

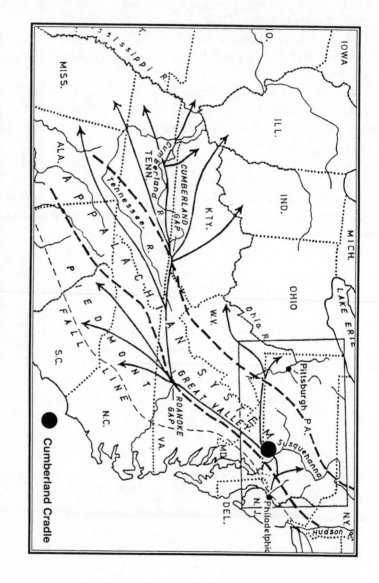

Centering on Philadelphia, the Cumberland Cradle was the seed bed of Scots-Irish migration to the Cumberland Valley.

11

John Dunlap, *the patriot printer*

American pioneer printer John Dunlap who printed the first copies of the Declaration of Independence was born in Strabane, Co Tyrone and lived with his uncle William, also a printer, in Philadelphia after his emigration as a young man.

Dunlap was printer to the American Continental Congress throughout the Revolutionary War and, in 1777, he founded the Philadelphia Packet newspaper, which he published daily after 1783. He was a close associate of Charles Thomson, the Ulster-born secretary of the Continental Congress.

As a soldier, John Dunlap served in the first troop of the Philadelphia Calvary, which acted as a bodyguard to General George Washington at the battles of Trenton and Princeton. He was a very generous man and personally contributed 20,000 dollars to supply the US army with provisions and clothing in 1782 during a crucial period in the War. He died in 1812.

A letter written by John Dunlap on May 12, 1785 to Robert Rutherford, a friend back in Ulster, urged others to follow him to America. He wrote: "The young men of Ireland who wish to be free and happy should leave it and come here as quickly as possible. There is no place in the world where a man meets so rich a reward for good conduct and industry as in America."

Strabane, where John Dunlap was born, is the part of Ulster described as "the emigration hinterland" of Londonderry and in 1780 his father was registered as a saddler in the town.

Soon after the Declaration of Independence was signed, John Dunlap's printed copies were circulated throughout various states and the first newspaper outside America to publish the first text was the Belfast News Letter, today Northern Ireland's leading morning paper.

Details of the Declaration had arrived in Londonderry by way of a ship from Pennsylvania in late-August, about six weeks after it was signed, and they were taken the 100 miles to the offices of the Belfast News Letter, then published by brothers Henry and Robert Joy.

For the News Letter, founded in 1737 and claimed today to be the longest existing English-language newspaper, it was a European scoop. King George 111 in London had not even been acquainted of the news of the Declaration - News Letter readers in Belfast were among the first to know on their side of the Atlantic, with the report carried in the edition of August 23-27.

Later in its edition of September 6-10, 1776, the News Letter reported on the unfolding events in Philadelphia:

"The 4th of July, 1776, the Americans appointed as a day of fasting and prayer, preparatory to their dedication of their country to God, which was done in the following manner: 'The Congress being assembled after having declared America independent, they had a crown placed on a Bible, which by prayer and solemn devotion they offered to God. The religious ceremony being ended, they divided the crown into thirteen parts, each of the United Provinces taking a part'."

The News Letter was an influential vehicle for relating news of the migration of the Scots-Irish Presbyterians to America during the 18th century. The paper carried many advertisements for the ship's passage from the Ulster ports of Belfast, Londonderry, Larne, Portrush and Newry to America, most of them carrying details of special provision for contracted labour in the new lands.

Conscious of the strong links between the Ulster and the American colonies, the News Letter kept its readers fully informed about developments affecting their kinsfolk across the Atlantic. Reports on various battles of the Revolutionary War, obviously dispatched on the various ships that kept moving regularly across the Atlantic, were carried.

12

Stamp Act that sowed *the seeds of dissension*

The 1765 Stamp Act which provoked so much hostility from the Scots-Irish Presbyterian settlers in the American colonies was designed to raise £60,000 a year from taxes for the Crown to pay off the estimated £350,000 cost of maintaining British troops in America.

The Act passed the British Parliament without debate and its Tory framers did not anticipate the hostility it would provoke, as they felt it necessary for the American colonists to pay for their own protection.

Americans, with the Scots-Irish in the vanguard, at first based their objections on the inability to pay, but moved to the more reasoned principle of "No Taxation Without Representation" and viewed the Vice-Admiralty enforcement courts as a breach of their civil liberties.

John Hughes, who was then Distributor of Stamps for Pennsylvania, in a report of October 12, 1765 stated: "Common justice calls on me to say, the body of people called Quakers, seemed disposed to pay obedience to the Stamp Act and so do that part of the Church of England and Baptists, that are not some way under Proprietary influence. But Presbyterian and Proprietary minnions spare no pains to engage the Dutch and lower class of people, and render the royal government odious."

The Stamp Act was the first direct taxation the British had introduced in America and, at a time when the seeds of revolution were being planted, it aroused opposition right across the colonies. Sons of Liberty organisations were set up to take action and the strength of feeling among the increasing patriot population was such that all of the stamp agents were forced to resign.

Georgia was the only colony where the Stamp Act was put into effect, albeit on a limited scale. In the other colonies the taxation courts closed rather than use the stamps and within a year the Act was repealed, largely due to the support for the American position by influential British statesman William Pitt and lobbying by Benjamin Franklin, who was then a colonial agent in London.

Franklin was sympathetic to the aims of the Stamp Act, largely influenced as he was by Philadelphia law associate and prominent loyalist Joseph Galloway, who was a leading member of the Pennsylvania provincial assembly.

Interestingly, Galloway in a submission held that it was the Scots-Irish Presbyterians who supplied to colonial resistance a lining without which it would have collapsed.

In a testimony before a committee of the House of Commons in London in 1779 he declared that at the beginning of the revolt not one-fifth of the people "had independence in view", and that in the Army enlisted by the Continental Congress "there were scarcely one-fourth natives of America - about one-half Irish, the other half were English and Scotch."

In 1780, Joseph Galloway, writing from personal observation of life in Pennsylvania, published in London his Historical and Political Reflections. This gave an inside history of the American Revolution, asserting that the revolt derived its formidable character from the organised activity of the Scots-Irish Presbyterians in Philadelphia and the frontier backcountry.

Galloway's analysis, however, was that the implacable Presbyterian faction could, by judicious means, be isolated and its influence so restricted that the struggle for independence would have to be abandoned.

He obviously wrongly reckoned that the Presbyterians and their allies had not the will-power to see their struggle through.

13

Charles Thomson, *the brains behind the Revolution*

The man who, more than anyone with the possible exception of George Washington, chartered the course for American independence was the scholarly Presbyterian elder Charles Thomson, who was born at Maghera, Co Londonderry in 1729 and as a 10-year-old emigrated to America with his family.

Thomson, acting largely behind the scenes in Philadelphia, was mainly concerned with shaping action, leaving the front stage to others. His commitment to the American patriot cause was unquestioned and, from he first took up the reins of office as secretary to the Continental Congress in 1774 until he stepped aside from the post 15 years later, the extent of his influence was manifest.

Known as the "Venerable Patriot", Charles Thomson was viewed as a man of sound judgment who had marked out a highly successful career as a teacher and classical scholar. His honesty and integrity was pronounced during the French-Indian War, when, after conducting treaty negotiations with the Delaware Indians, he was praised by the tribesmen as"Wegh-Wu-Whaw-Mo-Land" (translated - "the man who speaks the truth").

Thomson was selfless in his pursuit of the cause of independence, insisting he was interested more in results than in personal distinction. He was an astute political tactician; modest and tactful, with a complete insight into the manoeuvrings of the Pennsylvanian scene at the time, from both a patriot and British perspective.

When news arrived in Philadelphia in May, 1774 of a British bill to close the port of Boston, Thomson, along with another Ulster-Scot

Joseph Reed and the Quaker Thomas Mifflin, called a mass protest meeting which voted to commit Pennsylvania to joint action with the other colonies.

The three men would have been regarded as moderates and their action stirred others within the ruling Philadelphia establishment to stand up and be counted.

Thomson pressed for an immediate declaration in favour of the Boston patriots, to make common cause with them, and in the months and years that followed he became the prime mover in Pennsylvania for American independence and the proclaiming of liberty and democracy.

In his first year as secretary to the Continental Congress, Thomson refused to accept a salary, but such were the duties plus additional work in consultation and advice, and in order to provide for his family, he had to accept compensation. During his secretaryship, Thomson accumulated material which he embodied in an historical account, but he eventually destroyed this for fear that its publication might endanger the families of the leading protagonists on the patriot side.

Charles Thomson's signature was one of only two on the original Declaration of Independence of July, 4, 1776. The other was that of John Hancock, the President of Congress. In the political upheaval of the time, there was mass support for the concept of independence, but no great rush to sign the Declaration largely because of the dire personal consequences of failure.

John Hancock and Charles Thomson were the men who put their necks on the line and, in the wave of euphoria that followed in Philadelphia, others later appended their signatures.

American independence was actually signed on July 2, 1776 by the adopting of the resolution: "That these United Colonies are, and of right, ought to be Free and Independent States; that they are absolved from all allegiance to the British Crown, and that all political connexion between them, and the State of Great Britain, is and ought to be totally dissolved."

The rebelling 13 states of 1776 were clustered on what is today the eastern seaboard of the United States. Until the signing of the Declaration, eight (Virginia, North Carolina, South Carolina, Georgia,

Massachusetts, New York, New Hampshire and New Jersey) operated under a governor, council and officials appointed in London.

Rhode Island and Connecticut elected their own governor and Pennsylvania, Delaware and Maryland were proprietary colonies, where the proprietorial family chose the governor. All, however, were ultimately subject to the Crown, that is until hostilities began with shots fired at Lexington on April 19, 1775.

The resolution of American independence was presented to the Continental Congress in the signature of Charles Thomson, but the commemoration settled on July 4 as the day when Congress made its action public. Thomas Jefferson drafted the document and Congress directed that copies be sent to "the several assemblies, conventions, and committees or councils of safety, and to the leading officers of the Continental troops; that it be proclaimed in each of the United States and at the head of the army".

Charles Thomson sent a copy of the Declaration in his own hand-writing to the Scots-Irish printer he was acquainted with, Strabane (Co Tyrone) man John Dunlap, and one of the first printed copies was sent to the Committee of Safety in Philadelphia, which directed that it should be proclaimed at the State House on Monday July 5.

Patriot merchant and militia soldier Colonel John Nixon gave the first public reading of the Declaration in Philadelphia on July 8. Nixon was the grandson of Ulster immigrants.

A section of the Declaration contains the fundamental message: "We hold these truths to be self-evident that all men are created equal: that they are endowed by their creator with certain inalienable rights; that among these are life, liberty and the pursuit of happiness; that to secure these rights governments are instituted among men, deriving their just powers from the consent of the governed. Whenever any form of government becomes destructive of these ends it is the right of the people to alter or abolish it."

The copy of the Declaration to which signatures of Congress members were attached was engrossed on parchment under a resolution adopted on July 19, 1776. It was presented to Congress on August 2 and was signed by the members present.

Thomson worked closely with leading Whig politicians of the day Benjamin Franklin, Thomas Jefferson and John Adams and, after independence was declared, the four were authorised to design a seal for the new American state. However, their task remained unfulfilled six years on and Thomson, on his own initiative and with the help of a young Pennsylvanian lawyer William Barton, set about the design.

The mould of the seal was presented to Congress within a week and the inscription was written into law on June 20, 1782. From Thomson's original design emerged the Great Seal of America, which has since had artistic variations and six new dies cut - in 1825, 1841, 1854, 1877, 1885 and 1904.

One of Charles Thomson's last and most historic duties as secretary to the Continental Congress came in 1789 when, after the new federal constitution was adopted, he was delegated to convey to George Washington at his home in Mount Vernon, Virginia the request of Congress that he become the first President of the United States.

Charles Thomson's family roots were in the rugged Sperrin mountain region of Co Londonderry. The family had a farm holding at Gorteade, Upperlands near the town of Maghera and they worshipped in Maghera Presbyterian Church.

John and Mary Houston Thomson had six children - five sons and one daughter - William, Alexander, Charles, Matthew, John and Mary - and when his wife died at the birth of their last child, John decided to emigrate to America. He sold the family farm, and bade farewell to his friends in Maghera Church and in 1739 the father and his five siblings set sail from Londonderry.

Tragically, after a rough journey across the Atlantic which took its toll on many passengers, John Thomson died of fatigue as the ship was entering Delaware Bay.

The body was buried at sea to save the cost of a land burial and, unscrupulously, the ship's captain held on to John's monies deposited in the ship's safe at the beginning of the journey.

The Thomson children arrived on American soil as orphans, but managed to find placements in Philadelphia with kinsfolk and Charles started out as an apprentice blacksmith.

Through the generosity of a kindly and wealthy lady, he was sent to the new classical school at Thunder Hill, New London, Pennsylvania, where the tutor was eminent Ulster Presbyterian minister the Rev Francis Allison, from Leck outside Letterkenny in Co Donegal.

Charles graduated as a teacher at Philadelphia University in 1750 and 10 years later, he gave up this profession and moved into the mercantile business, and from there he developed a career in politics.

Charles Thomson was a deeply religious man and in retirement he spent most of his time on translations of the Old and New Testaments of the Bible from the Greek Septuagint version. There was a quite outstanding work, but few recognised its worth at the time and, regrettably, after his death copies were sold as wastepaper.

Thomson, whose first wife died in childbirth, passed away on August 16, 1824, aged 95. He was buried alongside his second wife Hannah in the family plot at Harriton, Pennsylvania. The couple were later re-buried at Laurel Hill, four miles from Philadelphia.

• A plaque marking the outstanding contribution of Charles Thomson as the "Venerable Patriot" in American public life is erected at Maghera Presbyterian Church in Co. Londonderry where he and his family worshipped before their emigration to America in 1739. The Thomsons had settled in Ulster during the 17th century Scottish plantation years.

"Let us raise a standard to which the wise and honest can repair; the rest is in God's hands"

Address by GEORGE WASHINGTON to the American Constitutional Convention in 1787, two years before he was appointed President.

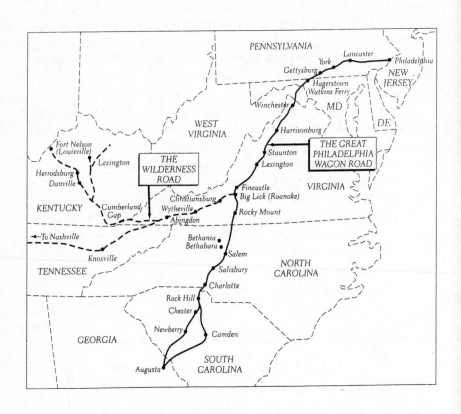

The Philadelphia Wagon Road and the Wilderness Road

14

Henry Knox, *George Washington's No. 2 in the Revolutionary War*

Genral Henry Knox, commander of the Continental Army and chief of artillery in the Revolutionary War, was a second generation Ulster-Scot, in that his father William emigrated from Londonderry to Boston in 1729 as part of the flow across the Atlantic at the time by Presbyterian families.

The Knoxes were Scottish lairds of Gifford near Edinburgh and William Knox's branch of the family settled in Londonderry and Co Down during the 17th century Scottish Plantation of Ulster.

They were involved in defending Londonderry for the Protestant settlements from the Irish Roman Catholic forces under King James 11 during the 1688-89 Siege.

William Knox, who became a wealthy shipmaster and wharf owner, married Mary Campbell in a Boston Presbyterian church in 1729 and they had 10 sons, with Henry the seventh, born in 1750.

Henry Knox joined the militia at 18 and, after witnessing the Boston "massacre" in 1770, he got involved full-time in the patriot struggle. He was a volunteer at the battle of Bunker Hill and at the Boston Siege and his courage and commitment to the patriot cause impressed George Washington, who appointed him colonel of the still fledgling Continental Regiment of Artillery.

Knox's artillery, when they got properly up and running, dealt a damaging blow to the British, leading to the evacuation of Boston, and they fought at the battles of Trenton and Princeton.

By 1777, the Continental artillery had developed from a poorly armed and inexperienced force to a well-organised and highly disciplined unit and Henry Knox and his men performed well at the battle of Brandywine. Washington's high approval of Knox continued for the duration of the War, with commendations at the battles of Monmouth and Yorktown,

He was appointed major-general in March, 1782 and six months later he assumed central command at West Point US army base, and succeeded George Washington as commander-in-chief during the period December 1783-June 1784.

In 1785 Knox became America's first Secretary of State for War, an office approved by the Continental Congress, and held the post during George Washington's Presidency until 1794. He pressed for a strong navy and Fort Knox was named in his honour.

Historians describe Henry Knox as being a man with outstanding administrative abilities, a loyalty to his chief and the patriot cause, and a sanguine outlook that made him a major figure in the winning of independence.

This father of 12 children died at the age of 56, peculiarly, when a chicken bone lodged in his intestines.

The East Tennessee city of Knoxville was named after General Henry Knox in 1791, after it was founded as a township by by Scots-Irish settlers who had moved from the Shenandoah Valley of Virginia and North Carolina. The surrounding Knox county was also named in tribute to the noble soldier.

A Covenanting Presbyterian family of Knoxes emigrated from Co Antrim to Charleston, South Carolina, sailing on the Earl of Hillsborough from Belfast in March, 1767.

James and Elizabeth Craig Knox and their young family settled on 450 acres of land at Boonesborough or Belfast township in the Carolina Piedmont and four of their sons John, James, Robert and Samuel fought with the South Carolina Continental line.

They were also at Charleston when the British attack came in May, 1780 and later fought at Kings Mountain. James Knox Jun. was killed a year later by loyalists avenging the defeat at Kings Mountain. A cousin, Captain Hugh Knox led the patriot militia in battles at Rocky Mountain, Hanging Rock, Congaree Fort and Kings Mountain

15

Ulster Generals *of the Revolutionary War*

JAMES McHENRY - SECRETARY OF WAR

James McHenry, from Ballymoney in Co Antrim, had a distinguished career as a soldier and surgeon during the Revolutionary War and he was imprisoned for a time by the British. His Presbyterian family had moved to Maryland in the mid-18th century and through the south eastern American states they made extensive settlements.

McHenry, who was educated in Dublin, helped run an importing and shipping company in Baltimore, then studied and worked in Philadelphia as a physician.

From his role as a Revolutionary War soldier, McHenry became heavily involved in politics and served as American Secretary of State for War during the 1796-1800 period under both President George Washington and President John Adams.

Fort McHenry at Baltimore is named in honour of James McHenry.

McHenry was an associate of Alexander Hamilton, the Secretary of the Treasury and George Washington's closest advisor in the fledgling American administration. The two men combined to thwart the polices of George Washington's Presidential successor John Adams and McHenry was forced to resign.

A Co Antrim Presbyterian associate of James McHenry was Blair McGlenachan, who was a banker, ship-owner and general merchant in Philadelphia and gave 50,000 dollars to the American War effort.

WILLIAM IRVINE - distinguished doctor and soldier

Brigadier General William Irvine, born in Enniskillen, Co Fermanagh, was another Ulsterman with a distinguished Revolutionary War service in George Washington's patriot army as a soldier and surgeon.

Irvine, a graduate in medicine from Trinity College, Dublin, was a surgeon on a British war ship sailing in American colonial waters during the Seven Years (French-Indian) War of 1756-63 and, at the end of hostilities, he doctored in a strong Scots-Irish settlement at Carlisle in eastern Pennsylvania.

There, he married Anne Callender, daughter of Captain Robert Callender, another Scots-Irish Presbyterian settler, and they had eleven children, five sons and six daughters.

Irvine was a member of the provincial convention in Philadelphia of July 15, 1774 which denounced British "tyranny" in Boston and he actively campaigned for American rights of independence.

In close liaison with George Washington, Irvine raised and commanded the 6th Pennsylvania Regiment (the Pennsylvania Line) at Monmouth, New Jersey. He was involved in expeditions to Canada and was captured and spent almost three years in British custody.

In March, 1782, he took command of the isolated frontier outpost at Fort Pitt (Pittsburgh), where, despite having depleted forces, courageously fended off numerous Indian attacks. He resigned from the Continental Army in 1783 and was appointed to purchase lands for the distribution to the Pennsylvanian militia veterans.

When the War ended, Irvine wrote to George Washington, complementing him on his success. Washington replied: "With great sincerity, I return you my congratulations."

Irvine was a Congressman over two terms (1786-88 and 1793-95). In 1790, he served on the Pennsylvanian constitutional convention and, in 1794, he acted as arbitrator and commanding officer of the state troops in quelling the whiskey rebellion in Pennsylvania, involving the Scots-Irish settlers.

He died in Pennsylvania in 1804, not before the Pennsylvania legislature rewarded his many valued services to the commonwealth by voting him a large tract of land on Lake Erie, known as Irvine's Reserve.

William Irvine's brother, Andrew, joined him on the Canadian campaigns as a lieutenant, and later as captain. Another brother, Matthew, was a surgeon's mate in William Thompson's Pennsylvanian rifle battalion until 1775, and surgeon of General Henry Lee's Dragoons from 1778 to the end of the War. Three of William Irvine's sons were army officers.

A grandson, William Irvine Lewis, was one of the 189 men who died with David Crockett at The Alamo in Texas in March, 1836. Lewis was a great grandson of Donegal-born John Lewis, the first Scots-Irish settler in the Shenandoah Valley of Virginia in 1732.

RICHARD MONTGOMERY - soldier on two sides of the American conflict

Richard Montgomery, the son of an Irish MP from Donegal, had distinguished military service in both the British and American Continental armies and he lost his life in the patriot assault on Quebec on January 1, 1776.

As an 18-year-old just graduated from Trinity College in Dublin, Montgomery became an ensign in the 17th Foot regiment in 1756, and within a year he was in the thick of the action of the Seven Years War, taking part in the siege of Louisburg in Canada.

As a lieutenant he took part in the successful British operations at Toconderoga, Crown Point and Montreal and in the West Indies he was at the capture of Martininque and Havana. On his return to Britain after the War he associated with leading Opposition Whig politicians Edmond Burke and Charles Fox and was greatly influenced by their radicalism.

However, Montgomery felt he had no future in England and in 1772, after selling his army commission, he headed back to America, then deeply embroiled in the early stages of the Revolutionary War. He settled on a 67-acre farm at King's Bridge, New York and married Janet Livingstone, of a prominent Scots-Irish family.

He accepted a commission in the Continental Army in June, 1775 and was appointed a delegate to the first provincial congress in New York. It was a big step for a man who for 16 years had gallantly worn the uniform of the British Army and, leaving his young wife, he headed north to become second in command to General Philip Schuyler in the Canadian invasion.

Montgomery assumed full command on Schulyer's illness and he showed outstanding military prowess in leading an offensive into Canada, despite having to cope with the inadequacies of inexperienced troops and serious logistical problems.

After taking St John's and Montreal in September-November of that eventful year, he pushed on to launch the unsuccessful attack on Quebec in late December and was killed in action on New Year's Day, 1776.

The British forces instantly recognised his body and ordered it to be "decently buried". In 1818, the body was transferred for re-burial at St Paul's Church in New York county.

Highest praise for this outstanding soldier came from London, from both his former friends and from his political enemies. Edmund Burke, speaking in the British Parliament, contrasted the "disgrace" of the large colonial army shut up in Boston with the movements of the hero who in one campaign had conquered two-thirds of Canada.

Prime Minister Lord North replied: "He was brave, he was able, he was humane, he was generous, but still he was a brave, able, humane and generous rebel."

Charles Fox retorted: "The term of rebel is no certain mark of disgrace. The great asserters of liberty, the saviours of our country, the benefactors of mankind in all ages have been called rebels".

The city of New York erected a monument to the memory of Richard Montgomery and a tablet was raised on the spot where he fell at Quebec.

Richard Montgomery was described as being "tall, of fine military presence, of graceful address, with a bright magnetic face and winning manners". He was one of the outstanding soldiers of the Revolutionary War, on either side.

ANDREW LEWIS - patriot general from the Shenandoah Valley

This Continental Army general was the son of Co Donegal-born Presbyterian John Lewis, reputed to be the first Ulsterman to settle in the Shenandoah Valley of Virginia in the early 1730s. Andrew Lewis, also Donegal-born and six feet tall with a very strong physique, was one of George Washington's leading officers during the Revolutionary War.

The Lewis family settlement was at Staunton, Virginia and, on his way to becoming the first military leader in the region, Andrew became militia lieutenant in Augusta county and a justice of the peace and, as a landowner, he amassed a considerable wealth.

During the French-Indian War of 1754-63, Lewis served alongside George Washington and took part in various expeditions against the Indians, at Sandy Creek (1756) and Fort Dequense (1758). He spent a time in captivity, but, on release, took part in important land negotiations with the Indians.

Lewis commanded 1,000 men in Dunmore's War against Shawnee, Miami, Wyandot and Ottawa Indian tribes in south western Virginia in 1774, winning a crucial victory at Point Pleasant. His brother Charles was killed in this battle and Andrew was appointed brigadier-general in the Continental Army in March, 1776, taking command of the units at Williamsburg, Virginia.

At Gwynn Island in July of that year, Lewis commanded action that forced the royalist Lord Dunmore out of the Old Dominion of Virginia. A higher command to major-general looked certain, but, when this did not come, an aggrieved Lewis resigned his commission, allegedly for ill-heath. He continued, however, to serve in the Virginia militia and on the state's executive council, chaired by Thomas Jefferson.

Andrew's older brother Charles served in the Virginia House of Burgesses and in the state conventions that ratified the Federal Constitution. Another brother William rose from lieutenant in the First Virginia company to major in the 10th and was captured at Charleston in 1780, with his release only coming when the War ended.

William's grandson, William Irvine Lewis, died with David Crockett at the Alamo in Texas in March, 1836. Other members of the Lewis clan distinguished themselves in political and military careers through the 19th and into the 20th centuries.

JOHN McKINLY - militia chief in Delaware

Ulster-born John McKinly was governor and militia commander in chief in Delaware at the height of the Revolutionary War and such was his standing within the American patriot movement, that when captured by the British he was evacuated to Philadelphia, away from his popular base.

This was in September, 1777 just after the battle of Brandywine, when the British were occupying McKinly's town of Wilmington. When the British left Philadelphia, they took him to New York county, where he was paroled a year later.

McKinly, born in the north of Ireland in 1721, had settled at Wilmington, Delaware after emigrating in the mid-18th century and, in addition to his practice as a doctor, he rose rapidly in local civil and militia affairs. He was Wilmington sheriff for two years and chief burgess for 17 years, posts which left him in charge of the militia.

In 1771, he was elected to the Colonial Assembly and, as brigadier-general, was instrumental in calling up the Delaware state militia and sending delegates to the Continental Congress. After his release in 1778, McKinly was elected to the Continental Congress, but he did not serve and spent the last 18 years of his life as a medical practitioner in Wilmington.

Courage was the mettle of "SCOTCH WILLIE" MAXWELL

General William Maxwell, "Scotch Willie" to his compatriots in the Revolutionary War, had a humble upbringing as a farm boy in New

Jersey after he moved to America with his parents in 1747 from their Co Down homeland in the north of Ireland.

Maxwell, a tall, ruddy-faced bachelor who spoke with a burr, had a chequered career as an officer in George Washington's army and, while his judgment and tactical ability in the field of battle was often the target of much criticism, his courage and commitment to the patriot cause could never be called into question.

His shortcomings as a general could probably be attributed to a liking for alcohol and, after the battles of Brandywine and Germantown in the autumn of 1777, Maxwell was charged with misconduct and was not exonerated, but at the November hearing the charges were unproved.

Maxwell joined a British regiment at the age of 21 and was on General Edward Braddock's expedition in 1755 during the French-Indian War. He rose from being an ensign to lieutenant in the New Jersey regiment and, during the final years of the war, took part in the attack on Ticonderoga and is believed to have been with General James Wolfe in the celebrated battle at Quebec in September 1759.

As a colonel Maxwell was subsequently on duty with the British commissionary department at Mackinac and, in 1774, he returned home as a veteran of 20 years military service to take an active role in the Revolutionary War movement in New Jersey.

"Scotch Willie" was a member of the New Jersey provincial congress in 1775 and in November he was commissioned colonel and raised the second battalion of the New Jersey militia. In February, 1776, he marched north at the head of five full companies in support of the ill-fated Canada invasion and suffered defeat at Trois Rivieres in June.

On return to New Jersey, Maxwell, as a brigadier-general, joined George Washington in attempting to resist the British troops at the Delaware River and was put in charge of four new regiments of Continental troops.

However, things started to go wrong during the preliminary manoeuvers of the Philadelphia campaign and Maxwell failed to arrive for the action at Brunswick, New Jersey in June 1777 because the order was not delivered to him. It was September before his troops went into action, at the battle of Gooch's Bridge.

Maxwell's main critic was Major William Heth, a veteran of Morgan's Rifles and it was a complaint from Heth which led to his trial. But Maxwell's army career continued and his men from the four New Jersey regiments took up arms at Valley Forge.

In May, 1778, Maxwell was involved protecting Washington's flank and he had a measure of success against the British at the battle of Monmouth a month later. He moved to protect the New Jersey coastline and then got caught up in an expedition against the Iroquois Indians.

Disillusioned with his role, Maxwell resigned his army commission in July 1780 and moved into less dangerous territory as a member of the New Jersey Assembly. He died in 1796, aged 63.

• Co. Down brothers Robert and James Maxwell took part in the Boston Tea Party in 1773 dressed as Indians. The Maxwells were members of a radical group called 'The Sons of Liberty' campaigning for American independence.

The Culbertson Family

This Co. Antrim family provided more officers to the Revolutionary army than any other family settled along the American frontier. The Culbertsons of Ballygan near Ballymoney were of ancient Scottish ancestry, and had been in Ulster since the early 17th century. In 1730 three brothers - Alexander, Joseph and Samuel Culbertson, from near Ballymoney, emigrated to Lancaster county, Pennsylvania. They settled in Lurgan, Franklin county, and called their settlement "Culbertson's Row", after the home of their ancestors in Ulster.

During the mid-1750s the Culbertsons migrated down the Great Wagon Road to Abbeville in South Carolina and there the families of James, Joseph, Josiah and Samuel spread out. Josiah served as a major and Samuel as a lieutenant and captain at the Battles of Kings Mountain and Cowpens. Robert and Joseph Culbertson, also listed at Kings Mountain, were engaged in the various Indian Wars.

16

Uncompromising Scots-Irish
in the Hornet's Nest

Charlotte, a North Carolina town settled largely by Scots-Irish Presbyterian families in the mid-18th century and ironically named for the wife of George 111, was described by Lord Charles Cornwallis, British commander in the Revolutionary War, as "the hornet's nest".

The ferocity of the Charlotte militia and the passion generated for the American patriot cause by the Ulster Presbyterian settlers was a factor which influenced the British in paying more than a passing attention to this rather troublesome region in the Carolina back-country.

It was quite significant that far more Presbyterian churches were burned to the ground then than places of worship for other denominations, and Charlotte, with its strong Presbyterian influences, became a moat in the eye of Cornwallis and his colonial associates.

Hawkins Historical Notices of the period recount that the Presbyterian Church suffered severely during the War of Independence -"Its ministers and elders went into the struggle for constitutional liberty with all their strength. Churches were destroyed, ministers and elders slain, congregations scattered."

The American colonial congress had long been worried by the anti-establishment feeling that was spreading through the Carolinas in the late 1760 and early 1770s. They prevailed on Philadelphia Presbyterian ministers to appeal to their North Carolina brethren to bear in mind that the dispute was over taxation without representation and there was no question of disloyalty or separation from the Crown.

A direct appeal evoked the proud memories of the Ulster Protestant stock: "If we are now wrong in our conduct, our forefathers that fought for liberty at Londonderry, and Enniskillen in King James's time were wrong. But we hope that such language will never be heard from the mouth of a Protestant, or from an English subject, and much less from anyone of our denomination, that have ever maintained the revolution principles, and are firmly devoted to the present reigning family as the asserters of the British privileges and English liberty."

This appeal had a measure of success over a large part of the Carolina up-country, but not in Charlotte, principal township for Mecklenburg county, where anti-British feeling was very strong. This was fuelled in 1773 by the refusal of the English Privy Council to grant a charter to the local Queen's College because of its Presbyterian non-conformist ethos.

The undercurrent of patriotism in the Carolinas led to a declaration of independence drawn up by community leaders in Charlotte fourteen months before the appearance of the July 4, 1776 document which confirmed the legitimacy and authority of the United States.

The conflict that erupted at Lexington and Concord in April, 1775 was also a factor in the hardening of opinion at Mecklenburg county and there was swifter reaction by the patriot class in this area than anywhere else in the 13 American colonies.

The radicalism that surfaced in Charlotte and Mecklenburg county was to a large degree influenced by the Scots-Irish Presbyterian clerics such as the Rev Alexander Craighead, the Rev David Caldwell and the Rev Hezekiah Balch.

Craighead, a nephew of leading Irish Presbyterian minister of the 18th century the Rev Robert Craighead, had long been in militant opposition to the establishment in the colonies, while his son-in-law Caldwell was in the vanguard of the struggle with his congregation.

Caldwell, born in the Scots-Irish stronghold of Lancaster county, Pennsylvania, absolved his flock from their path of allegiance, and closely studied the taxation problem and the charter of the North Carolina colony so that he could instruct them in their rights.

The Scots-Irish had been in the North Carolina territory from the early 1740s, when lands were opened up on behalf of the Crown by Lord Granville, and, it was through the colonisation a decade later by

Carrickfergus, Co Antrim man Arthur Dobbs and Granville's agent Henry McCulloch, that this Ulster ethnic influence became more pronounced.

Some historians claim there is not a document to confirm the existence of the Mecklenburg Declaration, and even Thomas Jefferson disputed its authenticity. However, a set of anti-British resolutions was drawn up by a Charlotte committee of leading citizens and militia men in May 1775, calling for the nullification of the authority of all Crown officials in the region, and swearing allegiance to the American Continental Congress.

Details of these resolutions appeared in the Raleigh Register and North Carolina Gazette in April, 1819 as part of an article by Dr Joseph McKnitt Alexander, whose father John was clerk of the Mecklenburg assembly. Dr Alexander insisted his version was a "true copy" of the papers on the subject.

It was said that the minutes of the Charlotte meeting approving the resolutions were destroyed in a fire in April, 1800 after being kept in storage for 25 years. However, not until 1847 was the precise narrative of the resolutions published, in a Charleston newspaper.

The 20 Mecklenburg resolutions stated, among other things, that all laws and commissions derived from British Royal or Parliamentary authority be suspended and that all legislative or executive power henceforth should come from the Provincial Congress of each colony under the Continental Congress. Phrases used, including the term "a free and independent people", later turned up in the text of the American Declaration of Independence.

The Mecklenburg Declaration resolved:

- "That whomsoever or indirectly   abetted, in any way, form or manner countenances the unchartered and dangerous invasion of our rights, claimed by Great Britain, is an enemy of this county, to America and to the inherent and inalienable rights of men.

- "That we the citizens of Mecklenburg county do hereby dissolve the political bonds which have connected us to the mother country, and hereby absolve themselves from all allegiance to the British

Crown, and abjure all political connections, contact or association with that nation, who have wantonly trampled on our rights and liberties and inhumanly shed the blood of American patriots at Lexington.

• "That we do hereby declare ourselves a free and independent people, and, by right ought to be, a sovereign and self-governing association, under the control of no power, other than that of our God and the general government of Congress; to the maintenance of which we solemnly pledge to each other our mutual co-operation, our lives, our fortunes and our most sacred honour."

Similar sentiments were expressed four months earlier - on January 20, 1775 - by Scots-Irish Presbyterian settlers at Abingdon in south western Virginia, close to the present state line with Tennessee.

In a memorial to the Virginia legislature the Abingdon settlers stated: "We are willing to contribute all in our power if applied to constitutionally, but cannot think of submitting our liberty and property to a venal British Parliament or a corrupt ministry.

"We are deliberately and resolutely determined never to surrender our inestimable privileges to any power on earth, but at the expense of our lives. These are our real and unpolished sentiments of liberty and loyalty, and in them we are resolved to live or die."

Another such resolution was the Pine Creek Declaration, drafted by a group of Scots-Irish settlers in a western part of Pennsylvania, 200 miles north of Philadelphia. This was issued simultaneously with the July 4, 1776 Declaration of Independence and, although the log cabin settlers were unaware of what Continental Congress politicians were doing in Philadelphia, the Pine Creek resolution was seen as an expression of support for the main document.

The hardy Pine Creek settlers squatted illegally on lands on the west bank of the Susquehanna River, outside the terms of the Land Purchase of 1768 and beyond the laws dictated from Philadelphia. Despite being "seated on doubtful territory", the settlers were not for moving and they formed a compact among themselves and established a tribunal known as the "Fair Play System".

Early in the summer of 1776, news reached this remote settlement that the Continental Congress might be about to declare for independence and the "Fair Play" advocates readily voiced their approval for a formal endorsement of their own. Thus, on July 4, 1776 they gathered on the banks of Pine Creek and, after lively discussion, they enthusiastically framed their local declaration.

The set of resolutions absolved the settlers from all allegiance to Great Britain and declared that they were henceforth free and independent. The Pine Creek declaration is viewed as a singular coincidence, action taken in the backwoods of Pennsylvania by a body of Scots-Irishmen, who, while not knowing precisely what was in the minds of the politicians and academics in Philadelphia, were of similar attitude.

The Pine Creek men went on to bravely serve as patriots on the battlefields of the Revolution and on December 21, 1784, the legislature of Pennsylvania recognised this service by granting the settlers the right to pre-emption to the lands they had squatted on before titles could be legally granted.

More than a year earlier, Scots-Irish settlers at Hanna's Town (Hannastown), Westmoreland county in south-western Pennsylvania had declared, on May 16, 1775, themselves publicly for the American patriot cause. They signified in the Westmoreland Declaration "a readiness to use armed resistance should our country be invaded by a foreign army or should troops be sent from Great Britain to enforce the arbitrary acts of its parliament".

Two Westmoreland battalions of militia were set up under the command of Colonel John Proctor and Colonel John Carnigan and took in the various battles.

Meanwhile, the Bill of Rights for the state of Virginia, heavily influenced at its drafting in 1776 by the Scots-Irish, declared that one of the inalienable rights of man is his right to worship God, according to the dictates of his conscience.

This bill led to the separation of church and state in Virginia and throughout the Union, but while religious liberty was a core ideal, Scots-Irish Presbyterian dissenters, particularly in the Shenandoah Valley, still laboured under the laws of toleration rather than being able to enjoy full religious freedom.

Under the legislation, dissenters were exempted from the tithe or tax paid to the Episcopal (Anglican) church, but it was not until the end of the War that Presbyterian ministers were given a limited right to perform marriages. The Presbyterian settlers, well versed in the separation of church and state by their ministers, were not a people easily staved off with mere toleration ahead of total liberty.

The 27 signators to the Mecklenburg Declaration in North Carolina, most of them Scots-Irish, were: Dr Ephraim Brevard, the Rev Hezekiah Balch. James Phifer, Colonel James Harris, William Kennon, John Ford, Richard Barry, Henry Downs, Ezra Alexander, William Graham, John Queary, Hezekiah Alexander, Colonel Adam Alexander, Charles Alexander, Captain Zaccheus Wilson, Weightstill Avery, Benjamin Patton, Matthew McClure, Neil Morrison, General Robert Irwin, John Flennigin, David Reese, Major John Davidson, Richard Harris, Colonel Thomas Polk, Colonel Abraham Alexander and John McKnitt Alexander, the clerk.

The reputed author of the Declaration was Dr Ephraim Brevard, of French Huguenot stock, with a grandfather who emigrated from Ulster with the McKnitt family.

David Reese's Welsh-born father, the Rev David Reese, was a Presbyterian chaplain at the Siege of Londonderry in 1688-89 and who later returned to Wales. David Jun. emigrated to America as a 15-year-old and married Susan Polk, of the family of President James Knox Polk. He was magistrate and a county court judge and a main purchaser of firearms for the Mecklenburg militia.

Although adopted by the Charlotte committee, the resolutions were never presented to the Continental Congress, thus their non-appearance in official manuscripts. But the flag and the Great Seal of the state of North Carolina carries to this day the legend "May 20, 1775", reputed date of the drawing up of the Charlotte resolutions. May 31, 1775 has also been recorded as the date of the resolutions, but the difference can be explained in terms of the old and new calendar.

Colonel Abraham Alexander and Colonel Thomas Polk, of first generation Ulster immigrant families from Londonderry-Donegal, led the debate for the declaration as representatives of Mecklenburg county to the North Carolina legislature.

Abraham Alexander presided at the Mecklenburg Convention which started on May 20, 1775 (the resolutions were signed at midnight on this date!) and he was active throughout the Revolutionary War, as a magistrate and militia leader.

Thomas Polk, a great uncle of American President of 1845-49 James Knox Polk, was joined in the militia by his younger brother Ezekiel, the President's grandfather, and, like Abraham Alexander, they became a thorn in the flesh of Cornwallis and his Redcoat army.

Other leading citizens of Scots-Irish lineage prominent in Mecklenburg county in the decisive mid-1770s period were the Captain James Jack, the Rev Charles Cummings and General George Graham.

The Scots-Irish Presbyterian clan in the Charlotte region was solid in its support of the American patriot cause and this uncompromising stance caused ire with the British forces, thus Lord Cornwallis's intemperate remark about the "Hornet's Nest".

Cornwallis found the North Carolina region around Charlotte, Waxhaws and Salisbury a much tougher nut to crack than the South Carolina Piedmont which he secured in 1780.

Defeat for his forces at Kings Mountain in October of that year forced Cornwallis to abandon his plans for North Carolina and this signalled the beginning of the end for British interests in the south eastern Appalachians.

The Crown position worsened at Guilford Courthouse, North Carolina in March, 1781, one of the bloodiest battles of the War. The patriots withdrew after losing 261 men, but Cornwallis paid a heavy price for a questionable victory, with 532 of his men reported killed, wounded or missing.

Six months later the game was up for the British colonialists when Lord Cornwallis's army surrendered at Yorktown.

•••

• In 1834, a North Carolina historian J. S. Jones wrote that the original Whig party of North Carolina comprised the wealth, virtue, and the intelligence of the province. This party, he said, carried with it the support of the Carolina back-country Presbyterian clergy, elders and people, who had been in the vanguard of the Revolutionary War struggle.

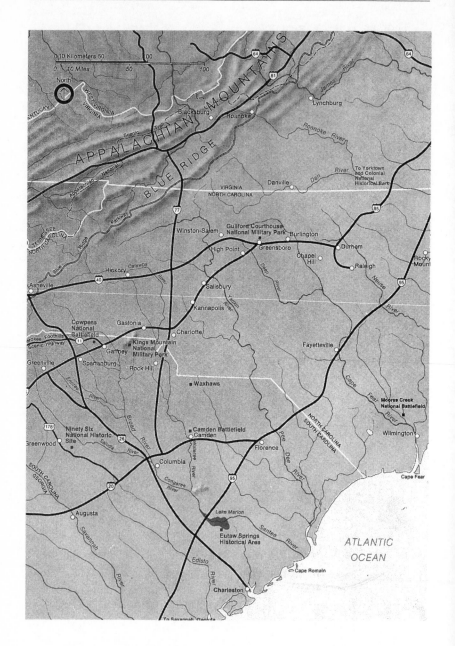

The Carolina backcountry battlefields of the Revolutionary War.

17

Hazards of *frontier militia life*

The patriot militia during the Revolutionary War was an all-embracing institution on the American frontier, particularly in states like Tennessee and Kentucky which were just being explored and settled by Scots-Irish families from Pennsylvania, Virginia, the Carolinas and Georgia.

War pension records from militia personnel in East Tennessee at the time provide an insight into how the backwoods militia was constructed and viewed by those from the frontier settlements who readily volunteered for service.

Every able-bodied man on the heavily influenced Scots-Irish settlements was required to go into militia action, armed with a long rifle, the muzzle-loading, flintlock firearm which was modified from a short, large-bore rifle.

Each considered himself a soldier, ready to join his fellows at short notice in an emergency, to defend both his family and community, from Indian attack, or from British colonial forces not friendly disposed to those who refused to accept their diktats.

Until the period of the revolution, the colonial wars in America were fought by British regulars, reinforced by American militia, known as "Provincials", recruited largely from the settlements of European immigrants such as the English, Germans, Dutch, Scottish highlanders and, indeed, a significant number of Scots-Irish.

The patriot militia units, which engaged in the battles of Lexington and Concord and were in service during the Boston Siege, and fought at Bunker Hill, formed the nucleus of the American Continental Army.

Militia service had a long tradition in the American colonies from the middle to late 17th century and most townships had a "muster field" where citizen soldiers assembled at designated times for rifle training and general defence duties. Their effectiveness as a force with quick manoeuverability and capability for swift, decisive action worked to the advantage of the American patriots in the Revolutionary War.

However, the part-time nature of the militia units meant that they could not always be relied upon to endure for long periods at a time. In one instance during the Revolutionary War, only a quarter of the 8,000 men in militia regiments serving under George Washington at Long Island in August, 1776 were still present when the battle ended.

Washington fully realised the limitations of the militia, and, reporting to the Continental Congress in a letter on August, 1776, he concluded: "If I were called upon to declare on oath, whether the militia had been most serviceable or hurtful, I should subscribe to the latter." Washington, however, was later to record his gratitude to the militia for the outstanding contribution they made in the winning of the War for the patriots.

American historian Claude H. Van Tyne in an interesting observation on the patriot militia of the Revolutionary War said: "Fortunately, for America's success, its army was not merely the armed and disciplined force, obedient throughout the years of war to its patriot leaders, but the ill-trained farmers, citizens, shopkeepers, ready to leave their work and fight when the enemy approached, and forming at all times a potential force far beyond the army in being. It was a nebulous, incalculable and very occasionally a mighty force".

The composition of the American patriot militia confounded the full-time British Redcoat soldiers. One British officer wrote of the assault on Quebec: "You can have no conception what kind of man composed the (American) officers. Of those we took, one major was a blacksmith, another a hatter."

The militia was "incalculable" in that it could never be counted upon by its friends, but equally could never be ignored by its enemies. The patriot militia, with the Scots-Irish in the front line of battle, defeated the British at Lexington, Concord, Saratoga, Kings Mountain and Cowpens.

Significantly, in these battles the militia units were led by experienced officers, who managed to inspire them to fight like regular soldiers, with techniques that were ideally suited to the forest and mountian terrains of the frontier backcountry.

Because of their pacifist convictions, settlers from the Quakers, Mennonite and Amish faiths were exempt from military service, while arrangements were made in Virginia for Methodists and Baptists to serve under their own officers in the local militia units.

Some militia groups in the Carolina Piedmont were loyal to the British Crown, but elsewhere they generally ended up on the patriot side.

The frontier militia men were not attached to a regiment in the established military sense and the mountain, river and bush warfare in the Tennessee and Kentucky territories was largely independent of the main battle theatres of the Revolutionary War of the eastern seaboard.

Militia service extended from three to nine months at a time, resulting in the sturdy backwoods farmers and hunters having to leave their families and farms unprotected for long stretches. Periodically, they were allowed to return home to put in crops in their fields, and tend to their livestock.

Very often, the consequences for women and children being left virtually unprotected on the frontier were dire and many militia men returned home from service to find loved ones brutally massacred and their homesteads destroyed in Indian attacks.

Tennessee historian Wayne C. Moore observed that frontier warfare was, by its very nature, terroristic. "It was designed to break the Indians' will to fight, or, conversely, to destroy the whites' determination to persist in their frontier settlements," he pointed out.

Frontier militiamen, paradoxically, adapted much of the fighting tactics of the Indian tribes they were confronting and, on their own familiar homeland terrain, they used these to good effect against the British Redcoat regiments in decisive Revolutionary War battles like Kings Mountain in North Carolina. Patriot militia commanders led their men into battle, doggedly urging them to give the enemy "Indian play".

From behind bushes and in deep undergrowth, through rivers and over mountain tops, they relentlessly tracked the enemy, destroyed their food and armament supplies, and laid ambushes and conducted their campaigns with a determined "eye-for-an-eye" retribution.

As they strove tirelessly to maintain their defences on the frontier, a clannish bond developed among the settlers (Scots-Irish, English, Pennsylvania Dutch, Scottish Highlanders and Welsh!) which brokered no division.

Few transgressions by the Indians against the white settlements in the 18th century Appalachian territory went unpunished.

Militia duty took the frontiersmen hundreds of miles from their homes, very often into neighbouring but hitherto unknown and unexplored states, and they had an exploratory eye to their duties when viewing with awe large stretches of good fertile land that so far had lay uninhabited.

Many readily returned to these lush regions with their families and kinsfolk to settle the lands when their militia duties were ended. Tennessee and Kentucky were settled in this way after the Revolutionary War.

Payment for militia service, depending on rank and length of service, was in most cases conducted by the allocation of sizeable land grants in the new territories being opened up in Tennessee and Kentucky, west to the Mississippi and beyond.

Militia life brought its dangers for the settler frontier farmers cum soldiers, but there were considerable dividends for those who survived the hostilities in the bitter Indian campaigns and the Revolutionary War battles.

> *"The Scots-Irish held the valley between the Blue Ridge and the North Mountain and they formed a barrier which none could venture to leap."*
>
> UNITED STATES PRESIDENT,
> THOMAS JEFFERSON
> (1801-09)

18

The Waxhaws and Andrew Jackson's
family War effort

Scots-Irish settlements of the Waxhaws region close to Charlotte in North Carolina where President Andrew Jackson grew up became a hotbed of American patriotic feeling during the Revolutionary War with much of the passion raised by the excesses of British cavalrymen led by Colonel Banastre Tarleton.

The defining moment for many backcountry Scots-Irish farmers, who until then had not taken sides between American and British interests in the War, came on May 29, 1780 in an incident known as Buford's Massacre.

The 350-strong 11th Virginia Regiment, led by Colonel Abraham Buford, was retreating back to their home state when they were ambushed at Waxhaws by the Tarleton-led Redcoats, numbering around 270, and nearly obliterated in a savage and merciless attack.

Dozens of wounded men were treated in the nearby Waxhaws Presbyterian Church, where Andrew Jackson and his brother Robert helped their Co Antrim-born widowed mother Elizabeth stench the soldiers' blood on an improvised straw floor.

The attack caused bitter resentment amongst the frontier settler families, with Tarleton, a Liverpool-born English aristocrat who later became a Tory MP, being despised as "a butcher". It resulted in many farmers and their sons queuing up to enrol in militia units that were soon to go into action at the battles of Kings Mountain and Cowpens.

An uncle of the Jacksons, Robert Crawford, was a major in the militia and the teenage boys' eagerness to get involved as patriots in the War was given impetus after witnessing the retreat of General Horatio Gates and his men on the road towards Charlotte after General Lord Charles Cornwallis's victory at the battle of Camden.

The Jackson boys were among 40 local militiamen gathered at Waxhaws Presbyterian Church on April 9, 1781 when a company of British dragoons attacked them with sabres drawn. Eleven of the 40 were captured and the church burned down.

Andrew, then only 14, tried to escape on horseback with his cousin Lieutenant Thomas Crawford, but they were pursued by the dragoons and captured. In detention, Andrew was ordered to clean the boots of a British officer, but he refused, stating he expected the treatment normally accorded a prisoner of war.

Incensed by what he saw as a defiant act of insubordination by a teenager, the officer then used his sword to strike Andrew's left hand and forehead, leaving a scalp on both which he carried for the rest of his life.

The British then ordered Andrew to lead them to the house of a patriot sympathiser called Thompson, but by taking a roundabout route this allowed Thompson to escape. As punishment, Andrew, brother Robert and 20 other militiamen were forced to march 40 miles without food and water to Camden, where they were confined to prison on a strict diet of bread and water.

Smallpox was detected in the prison stockade and Elizabeth Jackson persuaded the British commander to include her sons in an exchange of prisoners. Robert Jackson, however, never recovered from injuries received in the fighting at Waxhaws and died.

Elizabeth and young Andrew were distraught, but she felt the need to travel the 160 miles to Charleston to nurse American soldiers imprisoned by the British there.

A few months later she died with others from a cholera fever that engulfed the prison ship and was buried in an unrecorded grave at a spot known as Charles Town Neck. Her small bundle of possessions were sent to son Andrew at the Waxhaws.

Andrew, whose Ulster emigrant father Andrew died just before he was born in 1767, was now alone. His eldest brother Hugh died while fighting for the American patriot cause and now the War had claimed the lives of his mother and other brother.

American losses in the Buford massacre were 113 killed and 203 captured, but Colonel Buford and several dozen mounted men escaped. It was a well-planned operation by Tarleton, who recorded his casualties as 19 men and 31 horses killed or wounded.

For all the professional militarism of his victory and being labelled a hero by his own side, Banastre Tarleton lost the propaganda battle in American minds when details emerged that he had allowed "no quarter" even in death for the defeated patriots.

"The demand for quarters was at once found to be in vain; not a man was spared and it was the concurrent testimony of all the survivors that for fifteen minutes after every man was prostrate they went over the ground plunging their bayonets into each one that exhibited any signs of life," was one American account of the massacre.

In American revolutionary folklore Lieutenant Colonel Banastre Tarleton became known as "Bloody Tarleton", and "Tarleton's Quarter" - a cynical term for "no quarter" - was coined after that ill-fated battle at the strongly Scots-Irish influenced Waxhaws and Charlotte area which strengthened the resolve of the patriots to resist.

One Ulsterman who was at Charlotte with his family at the time was Patrick Jack, who emigrated in 1762 from a farm at Ardstraw in the Sperrin mountain region of Co Tyrone.

Patrick Jack first settled at Chambersburg, Pennsylvania before moving along the Great Wagon Road to North Carolina and he and his five sons were active participants as militiamen in the Revolutionary War.

The Jacks were continually on a wanted list by the British forces and the family home at Charlotte was burned by forces led by Banastre Tarleton in the hunt for Patrick Jack, who hid in a surrounding forest.

James Jack, a nephew of Patrick, was killed in the Revolutionary War and his 17-year-old son James took his place in the battle lines. James and Jeremiah Jack are listed as revolutionary patriots at the Battle of Kings Mountain in October, 1780.

•••

• Andrew Jackson Sen. and his wife Elizabeth Hutchinson emigrated to America with their young sons Hugh and Robert in 1765, leaving their home at Boneybefore near Carrickfergus, Co Antrim and sailing from the nearby port of Larne to Philadelphia.

They were of Presbyterian families who moved from lowland Scotland to Co. Antrim during the 17th century Scottish Plantation years in Ulster and worked as cottage linen weavers.

Jackson kinsmen were prominent citizens in the borough of Carrickfergus, an historic Ulster town where King William III landed with his army in June, 1690 before heading to the Battle of the Boyne where he defeated the forces of King James II.

Carrickfergus was also the home of North Carolina Governor Arthur Dobbs, who was instrumental in settling many Scots-Irish families in the colony.

The Jacksons initially settled at Lancaster county, Pennsylvania before moving to 200 acres of land at Twelve Mile Creek in the Waxhaws region of North Carolina.

Andrew Jun. was born at Waxhaws on March 15, 1767, a few weeks after his father's death. He moved on to become the seventh President of the United States, serving two terms in Washington during the period 1829-37.

Quite apart from his Revolutionary War experiences in his earlier life, Andrew Jackson became an American hero leading the nation's army at the Battle of New Orleans in 1815 and in the conquest of the Florida territory.

The Revolutionary War was a traumatic period in Andrew Jackson's life. He may have felt like a patriot and a hero, but through the War years he experienced hardship, pain, disease, wounds to his head and hands, and grief from the deaths of three of his immediate family.

Jackson emerged from the War a young man burdened with sorrow and deep-seated depression. He considered himself a participant "in the struggle for our liberties" and he never forgot the price that he and others had paid to secure them.

His deep American patriotic and nationalistic convictions remained with him for the rest of his life.

19

Ulster patriots at *George Washington's side*

JOHN ARMSTRONG:

This highly distinguished soldier of provincial Pennsylvania from Carlisle township was a militia commander in the expedition against Fort Duquense during the French-Indian War and in February 1775 he was the first patriot brigadier-general to be appointed by the Continental Congress.

Ulster-born Colonel Armstrong, who served two terms in Congress - 1779-80 and 1787-88 - recruited his men almost entirely from the Scots-Irish settlements of Cumberland, Lancaster and Dauphin counties and his French-Indian War expedition was the first offensive against the Indians in Pennsylvania.

Armstrong assembled 300 men at Fort Shirley on the Juniata River in August, 1756, and made rapid progress towards the Indian stronghold of Kittanning on the Allegheny River. The Indians were taken by surprise and decisively defeated, with more than 50 of the tribe killed. Casualties among Armstrong's men were minimal.

The region echoed with praises of Armstrong and his men, with the Colonel being honoured by the corporation in Philadelphia. The Indian threat had subsided and a greater sense of security prevailed.

In the expedition against Fort Duquense in 1758 led by General John Forbes, John Armstrong had 2,700 militia men under his command and his close friend George Washington a similar number.

Of this force from Pennsylvania, the Scots-Irish mustered the greater part of the contingent and their heroism led to the capture of Fort Duquense and the expulsion of the French from Pennsylvanian soil.

John Armstrong took part in the successful defence of Charleston in June, 1776 in his role as commander of South Carolina forces and at Brandywine in September, 1777 he was in charge of the Pennsylvania militia, before moving on to Germantown a month later. He graduated to major-general in 1778 and held this militia rank for the rest of the War. He died in 1795, aged 78.

A son, Major John Armstrong Jun., was also a Revolutionary War soldier, serving at Saratoga in October, 1777. After the Revolution, he entered politics and was a United States Senator in 1800-04, Minister to France in 1804-10 and Secretary of War under President James Madison in 1813-14.

John Armstrong Jun. was blamed for the failure of the US expedition against Montreal and for the British capture of Washington and was forced to resign. He retired to become an author, completing works on the War of 1812 and biographies on Revolutionary War generals Richard Montgomery and Anthony Wayne.

ANDREW CALDWELL:

This naval man of Ulster stock was commander of the Pennsylvania navy and commanded the fleet which repelled the British war ships Roebuck and Liverpool in 1776.

The Caldwell clan, some of whom were closely related in marriage to American Vice-President and leading South Carolina statesman John C. Calhoun, made outstanding contributions during the Revolutionary War on several fronts.

The Rev James Caldwell, son of Donegal-born Major William Caldwell, was known as "the fighting parson" in the Revolutionary War. This Princeton College-educated cleric was minister of the First Presbyterian Church at Elizabethton, New Jersey.

In the Carolina backcountry, Belfast-born John Caldwell, who emigrated with his parents to America in 1760, was a militia soldier and scout and fought at the battles of Kings Mountain and Cowpens.

Other Caldwells listed in these battles were Samuel, William and Thomas.

The Caldwells of Newberry, South Carolina, were active patriots in the War, and Major John Caldwell was killed. His bothers, James and William, both militia captains, fought at Cowpens.

JOHN COCHRAN

This medical director of the Continental Army at the time of the Revolutionary War was the son of Ulster parents from Co Armagh who settled at Sadsbury in eastern Pennsylvania.

John Cochran received his education under the tutorship of Donegal-born Presbyterian cleric the Rev Francis Allison and he entered the British service as a surgeon's mate during the French and Indian War of 1754-63.

Cochran helped establish the New Jersey Medical Society and when the Revolutionary War started, with others, he prepared the plans for reorganising the Continental Army's medical department. George Washington was highly impressed and in 1777 he appointed Cochran as the Army's physician and surgeon general.

After the War, John Cochran settled in New York and, in 1790, President Washington made him commissioner of loans

A grandson, John Cochran, was a leading politician and he ran for the American Vice-Presidency in 1864. He was also a brigadier-general in the Civil War.

MARGARET COCHRAN CORBIN:

This heroine, whose family suffered tragically from Indian attacks as a child in the western Pennsylvania frontier during the mid-1750s, performed heroics during the Revolutionary War and was given the colloquial title of "Captain Molly" for her militia service.

When Margaret was only four, her father, an Ulster-Scots pioneering settler, was killed by Indians and her mother taken captive. Margaret, who had been away from home at the time, was reared by an uncle and in 1772 she married John Corbin, a Virginian, who enlisted in the 1st Company of Pennsylvania artillery.

During an attack on Fort Washington on November 16, 1776, John Corbin was killed and wife Margaret stepped forward to take over his duties as matross on a small cannon near a ridge later named Fort Tryon.

Margaret bravely kept the gun in action, but was seriously wounded, with one arm nearly severed and her breast mangled by shot. With other casualties, she was moved to Philadelphia for treatment and later parole.

The Continental Congress recognised Margaret's heroics and, after being granted £30 for immediate needs, she was voted half-pay for life. Her contribution to the War was widely acknowledged.

GILBERT CHRISTIAN:

This son and grandson of Ulster Presbyterians who left Ireland for Virginia in 1732, earned his spurs as a Revolutionary War soldier in the frontier battles against the Indian tribes.

Grandfather Gilbert Christian (born in 1678 in Ireland) and his wife Elizabeth Margaret Richardson (born 1702 in Ireland) settled on the Beverley lands in Augusta county in the Shenandoah Valley about 1733. Their son Robert, who was also born in Ireland, was a recruiting officer for the militia in Augusta county during the Revolution.

Gilbert 11 commanded the Sullivan county (now part of Tennessee) militia and his prowess as an Indian fighter in the frontier region was legendary. He was in the front line in the battle of Kings Mountain in October, 1780, and was promoted to major and, eventually colonel, during expeditions to quell Cherokee Indian unrest.

Christian was a justice of the peace in Sullivan county, commander of the territorial militia, and the senate speaker of the state of Franklin, which dissolved after several years. His son Robert married the daughter of John Adair, the Co Antrim man, who raised the money to arm the patriot forces for the battle of Kings Mountain.

Colonel William Christian, uncle of Gilbert Christian, also commanded militia units in expeditions against the Cherokee and Chickamauga Indians during the Revolutionary War years. Their Holston River settlement of Christiansville is now the present-day north east Tennessee town of Kingsport.

SAMUEL FINLAY:

Samuel Finlay, of a Scots-Irish family, was a Revolutionary War commander of artillery and major of the cavalry in the Virginia Line. After the war he founded the town of Chillicothe, Ohio and was appointed by George Washington as receiver of public monies in the North West territory. During the War of 1812, he raised a regiment and served as general of militia

JOSEPH GRAHAM:

Joseph Graham was a militia leader in North and South Carolina during the Revolutionary War and contributed to the Mecklenburg Declaration of May, 1775 which preceded the Declaration of Independence.

Joseph, whose father James was an Ulsterman who settled in Pennsylvania in 1733, moved to Spartanburg, South Carolina in 1763 with his widowed mother and about five years later transferred to Mecklenburg county in North Carolina.

Graham was commissioned as lieutenant in the North Carolina Rangers and he was later promoted to captain in the 4th North Carolina Continentals. He distinguished himself in battle at Charlotte in September, 1780, receiving nine wounds. When he recovered, he organised a dragoon company with a role as major.

After the War, Graham became a successful businessman and, in his later years, he published letters and articles giving a personal account of the events which centred on the signing of the Mecklenburg Declaration. He also provided first-hand accounts of the Revolutionary War fighting in western North Carolina and in South Carolina.

CHARLES McKNIGHT:

The surgeon Charles McKnight was the grandson of the Rev John McKnight, an Ulster Presbyterian minister, and was recognised by George Washington for his outstanding medical service during the Revolutionary War.

Washington appointed McKnight senior surgeon of the flying hospital of the patriot soldiers and he served until 1782 before taking up a post at Columbia College, New York.

REV ALEXANDER McWHORTER:

This Presbyterian minister, born in Delaware in 1734, was the son of Hugh and Jane McWhorter, from Armagh. His father was a linen merchant and settled in Delaware in 1730 and later moved to North Carolina.

Alexander McWhorter studied theology under the Rev William Tennent, the celebrated long cabin tutor who was also from Armagh, and when the Revolutionary War began he strongly favoured the aims of the patriots.

In 1775, McWhorter was appointed to visit western North Carolina to try and persuade royalist sympathisers to join the American cause. On this mission McWhorter enjoyed some success and, by 1776, he visited General George Washington at Trenton, New Jersey to devise measures for the protection of the North Carolina state. He was present when American troops crossed the Delaware River and captured the Hessians.

McWhorter was chaplain to the brigade of General Henry Knox in 1778 and was appointed president of Charlotte Academy in North Carolina, but he left after only a short service due to the draconian measures of Lord Charles Cornwallis and his Redcoat army.

A committed churchman and Calvinist, he was active in arranging the Confession of Faith and Constitution of the Presbyterian Church of the United States.

GEORGE MATHEWS:

George Mathews, a post-Revolutionary War governor of Georgia, was the son of an Ulster immigrant who setted in the Shenandoah Valley of Virginia. George was a renowned Indian fighter and served through various battles of the War, taking part in the battle of Point Pleasant under General Andrew Lewis.

Mathews rose from lieutenant-colonel to colonel with the 9th Virginia company and he fought at Brandywine in February, 1777 and at Germantown in October of that year. He was captured and spent several months on a prison ship in New York harbour.

When he moved to Georgia in 1785, Mathews became militia brigadier-general and was elected governor in 1787. He represented the state in Congress in 1789-91.

In 1798, President John Adams nominated him to be the first governor of the Mississippi territory, but his name was withdrawn because of alleged dubious land speculations.

Mathews also got involved, independently of the US federal government, in territorial advances on the then-Spanish held Florida lands and in March, 1812, with backing from the English-speaking population in the region and volunteer recruits from the adjoining Georgia, he took formal possession of the township of Fernandina.

The action was repudiated by the US government and Mathews died a short time later. Interestingly, Florida became part of America seven years later through the Florida Purchase Treaty.

WILLIAM PATTERSON:

William Patterson, born in the north of Ireland in 1745, emigrated to America with his family in 1747 and he became a deputy and secretary to the New Jersey provincial congress in 1775. He led the Somerset battalion of minute men in exchanges in 1776.

ANDREW PICKENS:

Andrew Pickens, son of Ulster-born Presbyterian immigrant parents who settled in eastern Pennsylvania before heading south west down the Great Wagon Road, was a distinguished commander of the patriot militia in the South Carolina Piedmont region during the Revolutionary War.

This tall, lean, austere figure was a born leader and, while not noted for speech-making, he was a doer who, when he spoke, everyone listened. As an Indian fighter in the South Carolina back-country during the War, Pickens played a decisive role in thwarting the Cherokee assaults on the largely Scots-Irish frontier settlements there.

William Pickens and his wife Margaret, Andrew's grandparents, arrived in Pennsylvania from Ulster in 1720 with their six sons and Andrew's father Andrew married Nancy Davis, whose family had also moved from the north of Ireland.

Young Andrew was born near Paxtang in Lancaster county in Pennsylvania in 1739 and in 1740 the family headed to Augusta county, Virginia when the Shenandoah Valley lands were being opened up to Scots-Irish and German settlers.

By 1750, the Pickens were in South Carolina and Andrew married Rebecca Calhoun, a close relative of John C. Calhoun, who was American Vice-President over an eight-year period (1824-1832) to John Quincy Adams and Andrew Jackson.

The family lived for 10 years on 800 acres in the Waxhaws region along the Carolina borders and then moved to Long Cane near Abbeville in the south western part of South Carolina, where Andrew became a leading citizen.

To the Cherokee tribes, Pickens was known as "Skyaguusta", translated the wizard owl. They feared and honoured him as a battle leader who defeated them repeatedly on their home ground, but was a firm believer in fair treatment for the Indian nations.

Pickens was convinced the white settlers and the Indians could live harmoniously, each on their own lands, and he believed the treaties he helped to frame were just to both races. In later years, he expressed disappointment at the harsh way the Indians were treated by the white settlers.

When the war began, Pickens, father of six children, was a farmer, Presbyterian elder and justice of the peace, and as captain of the local militia he defeated local pro-British Tory loyalist and Indian forces at Ninety Six in 1775. There, he negotiated a treaty with the Tories that was later repudiated as the bitterness of the War hostilities increased.

Pickens rose to brigadier-general and, in February 1778 at Keetle Creek, Georgia, he demonstrated his tactical ability in charge of 300 men, who circled a 700-strong Tory force and won a significant battle which eroded British influence in the Carolina backcountry and led to the fall of Charleston and Camden in May 1780.

Pickens was captured by the British and later paroled, but when Redcoat forces burned his house he angrily broke the parole and rejoined the Revolutionaries. At the battle of Cowpens in January, 1781, Pickens rallied the militia to defeat the British and for this service the Continental Congress presented him with a sword. His son Robert also fought at Cowpens as a lieutenant.

Andrew Pickens was elected to the South Carolina state legislature in 1782 and that year he raised and commanded a company of 500 men, who in six weeks defeated the warring Cherokee tribes. He successfully negotiated an extensive land treaty with the Cherokees in 1785, a deal that was upheld by the U.S. Congress. He was a Congress man in 1793-95 and Pickens township and county in South Carolina was named in his honour.

The doughty militia leader lived until he was 78 and is buried at Clemson in South Carolina, with his tombstone identifying him as "a Christian, Patriot and Soldier".

Francis Wilkinson Pickens, grandson of Andrew Pickens, was a South Carolina attorney and member of the State House of Representatives in the 19th century. He was a U.S. Congressman, state senator for South Carolina and American minister to Russia in 1858-60. At the outbreak of the Civil War, he was Governor of South Carolina and, as a Confederate, demanded the surrender of federal forts in Charleston harbour.

OLIVER POLLOCK:

Oliver Pollock, a patriot supply agent during the Revolutionary War, was born in the north of Ireland and, at 23, he joined his father and brother in emigrating, settling in the Scots-Irish stronghold of Carlisle in Pennsylvania about 1760.

Pollock became a West Indies trader and in 1768 he moved to New Orleans, where he prospered as a planter and financier, working closely with the Spanish authorities.

When the War started, Pollock was behind a delivery of 10,000 pounds of powder to Fort Pitt (Pittsburgh) in western Pennsylvania and, despite strenuous efforts by the British to stop him, he was successful in sending vital supplies for the Western frontier operations of General George Rogers Clark.

By the end of 1777, Pollock had donated £70,000 worth of supplies on his own credit, and, when this was exhausted in 1779, he was forced to mortgage personal property to raise £100,000 and borrow another £200,000.

James Alton James, early 20th century author of the Clark Papers (The Life of General George Rogers Clark), wrote of Pollock's   financial backing for the patriots: "His amount surpassed the contribution of any other person to the direct cause of the Revolution".

By 1778, Pollock was commercial agent for the Continental Congress and procured goods from Spanish creditors for George Washington's army. Later, he also had a role in the capture of former Spanish territories held by the British at Manchac, Baton Rouge and Natchez.

Postwar, Pollock continued his highly successful commercial operations, but with the Continental Congress and the Virginia legislature slow to reimburse him for monies laid out, he spent 18 months in jail for failing to satisfy his creditors. However, when all his claims were paid back, he settled on an estate in Cumberland, Pennsylvania.

JAMES POTTER:

James Potter, born in Co Tyrone in 1729, was a leading militia soldier in Pennsylvania during the Revolutionary War.

Potter, who had settled with his family in Cumberland county, Pennsylvania, had been a commission ensign and lieutenant in Colonel John Armstrong's battalion in the French-Indian War of 1754-63. By 1776, he was colonel of the Pennsylvanian patriot militia and, within a year, brigadier-general.

He served on the outposts of Washington's army at Valley Forge and commanded the Northumberland county militia at the battles of Trenton and Princeton. In 1777, Potter was commissioned brigadier-general and fought at the battles of Brandywine and Germantown.

In politics, he was vice-president of Pennsylvania in 1781 and major-general of the Pennsylvania militia in 1782. He was also a member of the Congressional Council of Censors in 1784.

NATHANIEL AND DAVID RAMSEY

The Ramsey brothers made a highly significant contribution to the American cause in the Revolutionary War - Nathaniel was a soldier, lawyer and politician and David a physician, politician and historian. These sons of an Ulster Presbyterian immigrant from Co. Antrim were born in the Scots-Irish stronghold of Lancaster, Pennsylvania and both were educated at Princeton College.

Nathaniel Ramsey acquired an estate and law practice in Maryland and in 1775 he was a delegate from that colony to the Continental Congress. Within a year he was given a militia commission as captain of Smallwood's Maryland regiment, which eventually merged into the Continental Army.

Ramsey became famous for his role in checking the retreat of the American army at Monmouth, where he was wounded, left for dead and captured. He is credited with giving George Washington time to rally his army and is commemorated on the monument at the battle-field.

After his return to the Continental Congress (1785-87), Nathaniel Ramsey went on to become US marshal for Maryland and naval officer for the Baltimore district. His portrait hangs in Independence Hall, Philadelphia.

David Ramsey was a doctor in Maryland and Charleston and was a member of the South Carolina legislature for the duration of the War and his Continental Congress service was in 1782-83 and 1785-86. He was Congress chairman for a year and president of the South Carolina senate.

Ramsey was a federalist, who opposed the issue of paper money, easing of obligations on debtors and the importation of slaves.

As an historian, David Ramsey earned national distinction with his History of the American Revolution in South Carolina (two volumes 1785), History of the American Revolution (two volumes 1789), Life of George Washington (1807) and History of South Carolina (two volumes 1809) being best-sellers. After his first wife Martha Laurens died, Ramsey's second wife was Frances, daughter of the Rev. John Witherspoon, the signer of the Declaration of Independence.

David Ramsey, like his brother Nathaniel, was extremely proud of his Ulster Presbyterian heritage and famously stated: "No country gave us so many of our inhabitants as Ireland."

• Dr. James Ramsey, son of William Ramsey from Raloo near Larne, Co. Antrim, served in Captain Andrew Wagoner's company of the 12th Virginia Regiment in the Revolutionary War. The family had settled at Lexington, Rockbridge County in the Shenandoah Valley and Dr. Ramsey served for 22 years on the board of Washington College in Lexington, which was earlier known as Liberty Hall, but is now Washington and Lee University.

REV JOHN ROGERS:

This Presbyterian minister from Londonderry was chaplain of Heath's brigade in the Revolutionary War and chaplain of the New York provincial congress and the first state legislature in 1777.

Rogers was trustee of the College of New Jersey, afterwards known as Princeton College, during the period 1765-1807 and he was Moderator of the first General Assembly of the Presbyterian Church at Pennsylvania.

George Washington's First Cabinet

George Washington's first Cabinet in the initial United States Government of 1789 contained four members. Two of them were Scots, Andrew Hamilton of New York and John Blair of Virginia, and one Ulster-Scot, Henry Knox of Massachussetts.

Among the first Governors for the new State Government set up by the 13 colonies, nine (two-thirds) were either of Scottish or Ulster-Scots origin: George Clinton (New York), Thomas McKean (Pennsylvania), William Livingstone (New Jersey), Patrick Henry (Virginia), John McKinley (Delaware), Richard Caswell (North Carolina), John Rutledge (South Carolina), Archibald Bulloch (Georgia) and Jonathan Trumbull (Connecticut).

Presentation of the American Declaration of Independence to the Continental Congress, depicted in an engraving from John Trumbull's famous painting.

In CONGRESS, July 4, 1776.

A DECLARATION

By the REPRESENTATIVES of the

UNITED STATES OF AMERICA,

In GENERAL CONGRESS ASSEMBLED.

WHEN in the Course of human Events, it becomes neceſſary for one People to diſſolve the Political Bands which have connected them with another, and to aſſume among the Powers of the Earth, the ſeparate and equal Station to which the Laws of Nature and of Nature's God entitle them, a decent Reſpect to the Opinions of Mankind requires that they ſhould declare the cauſes which impel them to the Separation.

We hold theſe Truths to be ſelf-evident, that all Men are created equal, that they are endowed by their Creator with certain unalienable Rights, that among theſe are Life, Liberty, and the Purſuit of Happineſs — That to ſecure theſe Rights, Governments are inſtituted among Men, deriving their juſt Powers from the Conſent of the Governed, that whenever any Form of Government becomes deſtructive of theſe Ends, it is the Right of the People to alter or to aboliſh it, and to inſtitute new Government, laying its Foundation on ſuch Principles, and organizing its Powers in ſuch Form, as to them ſhall ſeem moſt likely to effect their Safety and Happineſs. Prudence, indeed, will dictate that Governments long eſtabliſhed ſhould not be changed for light and tranſient Cauſes; and accordingly all Experience hath ſhewn, that Mankind are more diſpoſed to ſuffer, while Evils are ſufferable, than to right themſelves by aboliſhing the Forms to which they are accuſtomed. But when a long Train of Abuſes and Uſurpations, purſuing invariably the ſame Object, evinces a Deſign to reduce them under abſolute Deſpotiſm, it is their Right, it is their Duty, to throw off ſuch Government, and to provide new Guards for their future Security. Such has been the patient Sufferance of theſe Colonies; and ſuch is now the Neceſſity which conſtrains them to alter their former Syſtems of Government. The Hiſtory of the preſent King of Great-Britain is a Hiſtory of repeated Injuries and Uſurpations, all having in direct Object the Eſtabliſhment of an abſolute Tyranny over theſe States. To prove this, let Facts be ſubmitted to a candid World.

He has refuſed his Aſſent to Laws, the moſt wholeſome and neceſſary for the public Good.

He has forbidden his Governors to paſs Laws of immediate and preſſing Importance, unleſs ſuſpended in their Operation till his Aſſent ſhould be obtained; and when ſo ſuſpended, he has utterly neglected to attend to them.

He has refuſed to paſs other Laws for the Accommodation of large Diſtricts of People, unleſs thoſe People would relinquiſh the Right of Repreſentation in the Legiſlature, a Right ineſtimable to them, and formidable to Tyrants only.

He has called together Legiſlative Bodies at Places unuſual, uncomfortable, and diſtant from the Depoſitory of their public Records, for the ſole Purpoſe of fatiguing them into Compliance with his Meaſures.

He has diſſolved Repreſentative Houſes repeatedly, for oppoſing with manly Firmneſs his Invaſions on the Rights of the People.

He has refuſed for a long Time, after ſuch Diſſolutions, to cauſe others to be elected; whereby the Legiſlative Powers, incapable of Annihilation, have returned to the People at large for their exerciſe; the State remaining in the mean time expoſed to all the Dangers of Invaſion from without, and Convulſions within.

He has endeavoured to prevent the Population of theſe States; for that Purpoſe obſtructing the Laws for Naturalization of Foreigners; refuſing to paſs others to encourage their Migrations hither, and raiſing the Conditions of new Appropriations of Lands.

He has obſtructed the Adminiſtration of Juſtice, by refuſing his Aſſent to Laws for eſtabliſhing Judiciary Powers.

He has made Judges dependent on his Will alone, for the Tenure of their Offices, and the Amount and Payment of their Salaries.

He has erected a Multitude of new Offices, and ſent hither Swarms of Officers to harraſs our People, and eat out their Subſtance.

He has kept among us, in Times of Peace, Standing Armies, without the conſent of our Legiſlatures.

He has affected to render the Military independent of and ſuperior to the Civil Power.

He has combined with others to ſubject us to a Juriſdiction foreign to our Conſtitution, and unacknowledged by our Laws; giving his Aſſent to their Acts of pretended Legiſlation:

For quartering large Bodies of Armed Troops among us:

For protecting them, by a mock Trial, from Puniſhment for any Murders which they ſhould commit on the Inhabitants of theſe States:

For cutting off our Trade with all Parts of the World:

For impoſing Taxes on us without our Conſent:

For depriving us, in many Caſes, of the Benefits of Trial by Jury:

For tranſporting us beyond Seas to be tried for pretended Offences:

For aboliſhing the free Syſtem of Engliſh Laws in a neighbouring Province, eſtabliſhing therein an arbitrary Government, and enlarging its Boundaries, ſo as to render it at once an Example and fit Inſtrument for introducing the ſame abſolute Rule into theſe Colonies:

For taking away our Charters, aboliſhing our moſt valuable Laws, and altering fundamentally the Forms of our Governments:

For ſuſpending our own Legiſlatures, and declaring themſelves inveſted with Power to legiſlate for us in all Caſes whatſoever.

He has abdicated Government here, by declaring us out of his Protection and waging War againſt us.

He has plundered our Seas, ravaged our Coaſts, burnt our Towns, and deſtroyed the Lives of our People.

He is, at this Time, tranſporting large Armies of foreign Mercenaries to compleat the Works of Death, Deſolation, and Tyranny, already begun with circumſtances of Cruelty and Perfidy, ſcarcely paralleled in the moſt barbarous Ages, and totally unworthy the Head of a civilized Nation.

He has conſtrained our fellow Citizens taken Captive on the high Seas to bear Arms againſt their Country, to become the Executioners of their Friends and Brethren, or to fall themſelves by their Hands.

He has excited domeſtic Inſurrections amongſt us, and has endeavoured to bring on the Inhabitants of our Frontiers, the mercileſs Indian Savages, whoſe known Rule of Warfare, is an undiſtinguiſhed Deſtruction, of all Ages, Sexes and Conditions.

In every ſtage of theſe Oppreſſions we have Petitioned for Redreſs in the moſt humble Terms: Our repeated Petitions have been anſwered only by repeated Injury. A Prince, whoſe Character is thus marked by every act which may define a Tyrant, is unfit to be the Ruler of a free People.

Nor have we been wanting in Attentions to our Britiſh Brethren. We have warned them from Time to Time of Attempts by their Legiſlature to extend an unwarrantable Juriſdiction over us. We have reminded them of the Circumſtances of our Emigration and Settlement here. We have appealed to their native Juſtice and Magnanimity, and we have conjured them by the Ties of our common Kindred to diſavow theſe Uſurpations, which would inevitably interrupt our Connections and Correſpondence. They too have been deaf to the Voice of Juſtice and of Conſanguinity. We muſt, therefore, acquieſce in the Neceſſity, which denounces our Separation, and hold them, as we hold the reſt of Mankind, Enemies in War, in Peace, Friends.

We, therefore, the Repreſentatives of the UNITED STATES OF AMERICA, in General Congreſs, Aſſembled, appealing to the Supreme Judge of the World for the Rectitude of our Intentions, do, in the Name, and by Authority of the good People of theſe Colonies, ſolemnly Publiſh and Declare, That theſe United Colonies are, and of Right ought to be, FREE AND INDEPENDENT STATES; that they are abſolved from all Allegiance to the Britiſh Crown, and that all political Connection between them and the State of Great-Britain, is and ought to be totally diſſolved; and that as FREE AND INDEPENDENT STATES, they have full Power to levy War, conclude Peace, contract Alliances, eſtabliſh Commerce, and to do all other Acts and Things which INDEPENDENT STATES may of right do. And for the ſupport of this Declaration, with a firm Reliance on the Protection of divine Providence, we mutually pledge to each other our Lives, our Fortunes, and our ſacred Honor.

Signed by ORDER *and in* BEHALF *of the* CONGRESS,

JOHN HANCOCK, President.

ATTEST.
CHARLES THOMSON, Secretary.

Philadelphia: Printed by John Dunlap.

117

THE DECLARATION OF INDEPENDENCE
46   *(Continued).* Fig. 117: Reproduction of the Declaration
as printed by order of Congreſs by John Dunlap of Philadelphia.

The American Declaration of July 4, 1776, as printed by order of the Continental Congress by Ulster-born JOHN DUNLAP of Philadelphia.

A commemorative plate issued by the American Department of State in 1819 bears the authentic signatures of the 56 signers of the Declaration of Independence. The names are surrounded by a border comprising the State Seals of the original 13 states and a view of Capitol Building in Washington.

The first public reading of the Declaration of Independence in Philadelphia on July 8, 1776 by COLONEL JOHN NIXON, an American patriot of Ulster parentage. Nixon was a member of the Philadelphia Committee of Safety in the period before the Revolution. Illustration by Edwin A. Abbey.

GENERAL GEORGE ROGERS CLARK,
Ulster-Scots Revolutionary War
hero from Virginia.

PRESIDENT ANDREW JACKSON, who
was in the front line of the Revolutionary
War fighting as a teenager in Waxhaws,
North Carolina.

The end of the American Revolutionary War: The Continental Army marching into New York. Drawing by Howard Pyle.

The Battle of Cowpens in South Carolina on January 17, 1781 where a large proportion of the Revolutionary soldiers were of Scots-Irish vintage. Drawing by John Andrew (1856).

'Dangerous Ground', an 1876 illustration by Julian Scott, depicts a group of American soldiers on patrol in Indian territory during the Revolutionary War.

*GENERAL GEORGE WASHINGTON,
the first President of the United States.*

*Co, Londonderry-born
CHARLES THOMSON,
Secretary to the American
Continental Congress 1774-
1789 and a close aide of
General George Washington.*

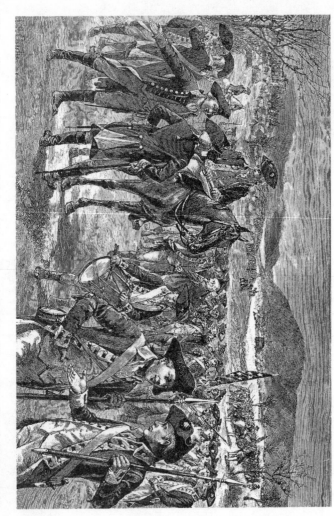

Disbanding of the Continental Army after the Revolutionary War at New Windsor, New York, November 1783.

THOMAS McKEAN, Delaware signer of the American Declaration of Independence and the son of an Ulster emigrant.

JOSEPH REED, President of the Pennsylvania legislature during the Revolutionary War and grandson of an Ulster emigrant from Carrickfergus, Co. Antrim.

JAMES SMITH, Ulster-
born signer of the
American Declaration for
Pennsylvania.

GEORGE BRYAN, a
Dublin Presbyterian, who
was Pennsylvanian
Vice-President during the
Revolutionary War.

The Rev. SAMUEL DOAK, son of a Co. Antrim-born couple and chaplain to the Overmountain patriot militia who fought at the battle of Kings Mountain on October 7, 1780.

MARY PATTON
1751 — 1836
One of that heroic band who
established a civilization in the
wilderness.
She made the powder used by
John Sevier's troops in the battle
of Kings Mountain.
Erected by her descendants
1932

East Tennessee monument to Mary Patton, powder maker for the Battle of Kings Mountain in 1780.

Gray's printing shop at Strabane, Co. Tyrone, where John Dunlap, the printer of the American Declaration of Independence in 1776, learned his trade before he emigrated to America in 1741. James Wilson, grandfather of President Woodrow Wilson, also worked at Gray's printing shop. He emigrated from Co. Tyrone in 1807. (Picture: The National Trust, Northern Ireland)

The centre of late 18th century Philadelphia, where the Scots-Irish were a very influential community. From Scharf and Westcott, History of Philadelphia 1884

His Excellency's ANSWER.

To the Yankee Club of Stewartstown, in the county of Tyrone, and Province of Ulster, Ireland.

Gentlemen,

It is with unfeigned satisfaction I accept your congratulations on the late happy and glorious revolution.

The generous indignation, against *the foes to the rights of human nature*, with which you seem to be animated, and the exalted sentiments of liberty, which you appear to entertain; are too confonant to the feelings and principles of the citizens of the United States of America, not to attract their veneration and esteem;—did not the affectionate and anxious concern with which you regarded their struggle for freedom and independence, entitle you to their more particular acknowledgments.

If in the course of our successful contest, any good consequence have resulted to the oppressed kingdom of Ireland, it will afford a new source of felicitation to all who respect the interests of humanity.

I am now, gentlemen, to offer you my best thanks for the indulgent sentiments you are pleased to express of my conduct; and for your benevolent wishes respecting my personal welfare, as well as with regard to a more interesting object—the prosperity of my country. I have the honour to be, with due consideration, gentlemen, your most obedient, humble servant,

G. WASHINGTON.

Mount Vernon, in Virginia, Jan. 20, 1784.

Letter of January 20, 1784 to George Washington from the Yankee Club of Stewartstown, Co. Tyrone.

20

The explorations and soldiering
of George Rogers Clark

G eneral George Rogers Clark, celebrated conqueror of the old North West trail on the upper reaches of the Ohio River, was a Virginian of Ulster Presbyterian family stock whose exploits as a surveyor, explorer and soldier gave him an honoured place in the annals of the Revolutionary War.

This red-haired frontiersmen with penetrating black eyes first came to prominence as a 20-year-old in the summer of 1772 when he explored down the Ohio River from Pittsburgh to the mouth of the Kanawha River with a group of adventurers.

In the following spring, Clark went on another expedition 130 miles below Pittsburgh which led to his involvement with the Ohio company in opening up lands in Kentucky for settlement.

When the war started, George Rogers Clark distinguished himself for the patriots in a number of battles and, particularly significant, in 1778, was his role in rescuing Kentucky frontier settlements under attack from British-backed Cherokee Indians.

After running the gauntlet of Indian ambushes over 400 miles of frontier territory, Clark and his long rifle comrades managed to get fresh gunpowder supplies to the settlers. He later led a force of 175 men from Virginia through 180 miles of swamp and forest in Illinois to capture Kaskasakia and Cahokia forts on the Mississippi River and Vincennes fort on the Wabash River.

This was a perilous campaign - there were no animals to kill for food - the floods had driven them away. At times the men were up to their shoulders in icy water and could only manage about three miles in one day. Their ammunition was soaked, but eventually they arrived to relieve the situation. As a result of this campaign, the United States, through the Treaty of Paris of 1783, obtained the lands north west of the Ohio River and Clark's sterling efforts considerably eased the pressures on frontier settlers in the upper Ohio River region.

The north west territories included the present day states of Ohio, Illinois, Indiana, Wisconsin, Michigan and Minnesota. Ironically, Clark and his men never received payment from the commonwealth of Virginia for this heroic service.

After the War, Clark, born in Charlottsville, Virginia, served on a board which supervised the allocation of 150,000 acres of land in the Louisville area of mid-Kentucky which the state of Virginia had granted for Revolutionary War veterans.

Along with Benjamin Logan, another Scots-Irishman, Clark conducted a campaign against the Wabash Indians and Shawnee tribes who were harassing the white settlers in northern Kentucky.

Clark's adventurous militarism in the north-west campaigns of the Revolutionary War and after years was not entirely appreciated by the American establishment and in some ways this made him sympathetically inclined in his later years towards French interests in North America.

In 1793, he wrote to France's United States representative Edmond Charles Genet: "My country has proved notoriously ungrateful for my services, but I still have much influence in the West."

This led to Clark accepting a commission in the French army, with the objective of attacking Spanish interests west of the Mississippi.

An attempt by Clark to found a colony in Louisiana failed because the Spanish Roman Catholic authorities there would not accept his demand for political and religious freedom.

A planned expedition in 1793-94 to take possession of disputed lands between the Yazoo River and the Natchez region in French Louisiana, with the help of 1,500 Kentucky and Tennessee troops, was halted on the instructions of President George Washington.

The United States demanded that he surrender this commission and he was forced to take refuge in St Louis. Out of favour with his own government, Clark built a cabin at Clarksville on the Indiana side of the Ohio River and, from there, he ran a gristmill and served as chairman of the local commission for apportioning land to veterans of his Illinois regiment.

By this time his health had deteriorated and, after moving to Louisville, Kentucky, he died in 1818.

Brigadier-general William Clark, younger brother of George Rogers Clark, was involved with Captain Meriwether Lewis in the celebrated overland expedition of 1804-06 from the Mississippi over the Rocky Mountains to the north-west Pacific coast region. This was ordered by President Thomas Jefferson, after the United States government had purchased the Louisiana lands for 15 million dollars in 1803.

The heroism of the Clarks - George Rogers and William - was aptly summed up by American author James Alexander Thom, when he said: "In one generation the Clark family of Virginia fought for our nation's independence and explored, conquered and settled the continent from sea to shining sea."

William Crawford's links with George Washington

Second generation Scots-Irishman William Crawford, who had a brutal death by Indians, had a long association with George Washington from their time together as frontier land surveyors in Virginia and Pennsylvania through to their frontline role in the Revolutionary War.

Crawford, belonging to an Ulster Presbyterian family which had settled the Berkeley lands of the Shenandoah Valley, was of the same age and temperament as Washington and over a number of years they joined on various expeditions in pursuit of new territories and met resistance from hostile Indian tribes.

They became familiar with the rich fertile region south east of Pittsburgh and it was in that locality in 1765 that Crawford built a log cabin and cleared 376 acres of land. A year later, he was joined by his wife and three children, to establish himself as an Indian trader, surveyor and farmer.

Washington and Crawford teamed up again in 1770 to travel extensively through the Ohio Valley, sharing their interest in land speculation by the selection and surveying of tracts of up to 40,000 acres. They collaborated with General George Rogers Clark, then engaged in his North West expedition.

When the War commenced, William Crawford was in command of 500 militia troops from the Pittsburgh area, mostly Scots-Irish, and their task was in thwarting Indian attacks on the western frontier of Pennsylvania and Virginia.

The close association with George Washington was maintained and, on the strength of his defence activities at Pittsburgh (then Fort Pitt) he was appointed lieutenant colonel of the 5th Virginian Regiment. He later became colonel of the 7th Virginia Line and led his troops into battle at Long Island, Trenton and Princeton.

George Washington regarded Crawford as "a very good officer" and highly commended his service in defending the frontier outpost settlements.

In 1782, Crawford was persuaded to head up an expedition to resist Tory-Indian offensives against the frontier forts and it was while on duty in the Upper Sandusky region that he was captured with others by a group of Delaware Indians.

Their capture had come after reversals by Crawford's militia at Sandusky and Olentangy. They were taken back to an Indian village and, after nine of his companions were tomahawked and scalped, the cruel torture of William Crawford began.

Agonised by the brutality inflicted on him over a period of several hours, Crawford pleaded with his Indian captors to shoot him, but to no avail. The long gruesome death was witnessed by Dr. Knight, the expedition's surgeon, who was also captured but somehow managed to escape and make it back to Fort Pitt after wandering through the wilderness for three weeks.

One of Crawford's officers, Captain William Caldwell, in a letter of two days later to his superior in Detroit, wrote: "William Crawford died like a hero; never changed his countenance tho' they scalped him alive and then laid hot ashes upon his head after which they roasted him by a slow fire."

★★★

21

Ulstermen who led the *Pennsylvania Line*

Colonel William Thompson's battalion of riflemen was one of the foremost regiments in General George Washington's Pennsylvania Line, composed mainly of Scots-Irishmen. This regiment, the first to be enlisted under the authority of the Continental Congress, formed the nucleus of the American army, with soldiers absolutely loyal to the patriot cause, purporting to "know no fatherland but the wilderness".

Thompson's men were recruited in pursuance of two resolutions of Congress, adopted June 14 and 22, 1775, which authorised the enlistment of nine companies of expert riflemen. Congress had originally stipulated only six companies, but so many volunteers presented themselves from the Scots-Irish settlements that another three had to be formed.

Seven companies of this regiment - the first, second, third, fourth, fifth, eighth and ninth - were composed almost exclusively of Scots-Irishmen; one, the seventh was made up almost entirely of Germans from Berks County, and another, the sixth recruited from German settlements in Northampton county,

The commanders, chaplains and officers of the regiment were overwhelmingly Scots-Irish Presbyterians, with the original command taken by the Ulster-born Colonel William Thompson, a surveyor and justice of the peace from Carlisle, Pennsylvania.

Thompson had served as a captain in the French-Indian War of 1756-63 under another Ulstermen John Armstrong and was involved in locating lands granted to officers on the western frontier of Pennsylvania province.

Other notable officers in Thompson's battalion were Lieutenant-Colonel Edward Hand, Colonel James Chambers and Major Robert Megaw. The regiment became the Second Regiment of the Continental Line, and after January 1, 1776, the First Regiment.

A military journal of the Revolution, dated August, 1775, commented on the appearance and marksmanship of the regiment: "They are remarkably stout and hardy men; many of them exceeding six feet in height. They are dressed in white frocks or rifle shirts and round hats.

"These men are remarkable for the accuracy of their aim; striking a mark with great certainty at two hundred yards distance. At a review, a company of them, while in a quick advance, fired their balls into objects of seven inches diameter at the distance of 250 yards.

"They are now stationed in our lines, and their shot have frequently proved fatal to British officers who expose themselves to view at more than double the distance of common musket shot".

The regiment took part in the Boston siege of 1775-76 and made a big impression with the New England Yankees, with their rugged appearance and shooting markmanship.

William Thompson moved on to command patriot forces sent to Canada, but, after a reversal at Trois Rivieres on the Hudson River, he was captured by the British and held for four years. He died in 1781, aged only 45.

Another regiment of Scots-Irishmen raised under the authority of the Continental Congress, on July 15, 1776, was the Eighth Pennsylvania. This regiment comprised seven companies from Westmoreland county, and one from Bedford county. The original purpose was to guard the western posts and to protect the frontier, but in the national emergency of 1777 it joined the Continental Army under George Washington.

The Provincial Convention of Pennsylvania on July 20, 1776 recommended to Congress for field officers of this regiment - Colonel Aeneas Mackey, Lieutenant-Colonel George Wilson and Major Richard Butler. The regiment was overwhelmingly Scots-Irish, from staff and non-commissioned officers to privates, with a Captain Sam Brady one of the most celebrated commanders.

Thousands of Scots-Irishmen from Pennsylvania served in the Continental Army and they were so numerous in the patriot ranks that General Henry "Light-Horse Harry" Lee paid tribute to them as the "Line of Ireland".

Pennsylvania soldiers from Ulster stock who gained distinction in the War included generals John Armstrong, William Thompson, James Ewing, William Irvine, James Potter, Ephraim Blaine, Joseph Reed, Andrew Porter, and Colonel John Nixon.

Irish-born Edward Hand, a surgeon's mate with the 18th Royal Irish Regiment of the British Army, came to Philadelphia in 1767 and served at Fort Pitt in western Pennsylvania. When the Revolutionary War began, Hand, a Philadelphia doctor by this time, changed sides to become one of the most respected officers in the patriot militia ranks.

Edward Hand joined Colonel William Thompson's Pennsylvania rifle battalion in the Boston Siege of 1775 and early in 1776 he was active in organising and drilling the Lancaster county militia associations in south eastern Pennsylvania.

By 1777, he was a colonel in charge of the First Pennsylvania regiment and on Long Island he was George Washington's main source of information as the British forces built up their strength on Staten Island. They saw action at the battles of Long Island and White Plains which helped Washington to victory at Princeton.

Washington was highly impressed by the "consistently fine" conduct of the "tough and deadeyed" Pennsylvania riflemen and he instructed Congress to appoint Hand a brigadier-general. Over the next few years, Hand commanded militia against the British and their Indian allies in western Pennsylvania and Ohio, with mixed fortune.

George Washington continued to admire Hand's sterling qualities as a soldier and in November, 1780 when Alexander Scammell resigned as assistant general of the Continental Army, Washington knew where to turn to.

Hand, at Washington's side in the battle of Yorktown, served until 1783 before returning to his medical practice in Philadelphia. As a strong federalist, he was also active in politics and civic affairs, being a Congressman in 1784-85 and in 1790 he signed the Pennsylvania constitution. He died in 1802, aged 58.

Ephraim Blaine, a doughty Ulsterman, was commissionary officer with the Eighth Pennsylvania Regiment and commander of supplies with the Continental Army in 1777. He was a commander-general at the battles of Valley Forge and Yorktown, in the frontline staff of Washington.

A descendant was James G. Blaine, the Secretary of State to Presidents James A. Garfield and Chester Alan Arthur and an unsuccessful Republican Presidential candidate in 1884 against President Grover Cleveland.

Joseph Reed, the grandson of an Ulster immigrant from Carrickfergus in Co Antrim and son of a wealthy Pennsylvania merchant, was another key figure in George Washington's Continental Army. New Jersey-born and London-educated, Reed came to prominence as a lawyer in Philadelphia and when hostilities commenced he was appointed lieutenant-colonel of the militia.

Reed eventually became Washington's army secretary and, with his exceptional intelligence and legal experience, he played an important role in the military and political aspects of the New York campaign of 1776.

Reed was elected to the Continental Congress in 1777 and was closely involved with Congress secretary Charles Thomson, who was born in Maghera, Co Londonderry, and Dublin-born Presbyterian leader George Bryan. He took part in the Peace Commission of Carlisle in Pennsylvania in 1778 and was president of the Supreme Executive Council of Pennsylvania. However, ill-health overtook him and he died in 1785, aged only 44.

General James Ewing, another of Ulster stock, began his military career as a lieutenant in the French-Indian war and from 1771 to 1775 he was a delegate to the Pennsylvania assembly from Lancaster county. On July 4, 1776 he became brigadier-general of the Pennsylvania militia in command of the second brigade and in 1782-83 he served as vice-president of Pennsylvania.

John Nixon, the man who gave the first reading of the Declaration of Independence in Philadelphia on July 8, 1776, was the grandson of Ulster immigrants. Nixon was not just a leading Revolutionary soldier in Pennsylvania, but a merchant and financier of high repute. He had little schooling before he inherited at 16 his father's lucrative shipping business at Philadelphia port and he became a lieutenant of the Dock Ward Company in 1756.

Nixon was one of the signers of Pennsylvania paper money in the 1760s and, just before the outbreak of the Revolutionary War, he presided over the provincial committee of safety when its leaders Benjamin Franklin and Robert Morris were absent. He commanded the defence of Fort Island in the Delaware region in 1776, as well as the Philadelphia guard, and after his public reading of the Declaration he marched with his battalion to the defence of Fort Amboy. He also fought in the Trenton and Princeton campaigns.

By 1779, Nixon was an auditor of public accounts and was involved in setting up and adjusting the American Continental currency. He helped organise the Bank of Pennsylvania to supply the Army, contributing £5,000 of his own money, and in 1784 he was appointed a director of the Bank of North America, and in 1792 its president. He was a Philadelphia city alderman in 1789-96.

The flag of the First Continental Regiment of Foot in 1776 (The Pennsylvania Line), initially commanded by Colonel William Thompson and later by Colonel Edward Hand. The flag depicted a deep green field, a yellow tiger in a crimson square, a hunter in white and a blue scroll.

*The Long Knife - a picture portrait of a typical Scots-Irish American
frontiersman at the time of the Revolutionary War.
Drawing by David Wright (Nashville), painter of the American Frontier.*

22

Scots-Irish evoke the spirit of Gideon
at Kings Mountain

The Battle of Kings Mountain in South Carolina on October 7, 1780 is recognised as a very significant turning point in the course of the American War of Independence and this encounter on the patriot side was fought and won overwhelmingly by a group of Scots-Irish militiamen known as the Overmountain Men.

British colonial forces suffered a major set-back in this battle and, after a second reversal in a battle three months later at nearby Cowpens, Crown rule in the American colonies effectively came to an end and independence was ratified.

The Overmountain men who had settled on the western Watuaga region across the Blue Ridge Mountains had become a thorn in the flesh for Crown interests in the inner colonies during the 1770s and the British commander Colonel Patrick Ferguson threw down the gauntlet to them and threatened to squash their defiance.

Ferguson sent a message to them "to desist from their opposition to the British arms, and take protection under his standard". If they did not, Ferguson threatened to march his loyalist army over the Blue Ridge, hang the Overmountain leaders and lay waste their country "with fire and sword".

Ferguson's message had the opposite effect: it inspired the Overmountain men to start preparations for anything which Ferguson saw fit to throw at them and they resolved, with heart and hand, to maintain their cultural identity and their independence.

The Overmountain men (Wataugans) were led by French Huguenot John Sevier, Welshman Isaac Shelby and two Scots-Irish Presbyterians William Campbell and Charles McDowell, whose families had settled in the Shenandoah Valley of Virginia and North Carolina.

Patrick Ferguson, a career army officer from Aberdeen in Scotland, was considered the top British soldier of his day and was the inventor of the first breechloading rifle. He served under Lord Charles Cornwallis at Charleston and as loyalist militia inspector of the Southern Province he raised a force of some 4,000, mostly from the Carolinas and New York, many of highland Scots stock like himself.

The Overmountain men, by comparison, were poorly equipped in arms, ammunition and resources and, according to accepted army manuals, were not considered a match for Ferguson's force. Colonel John Sevier tried personally to raise funds, but he found that the Wataugan settlers had mortgaged themselves heavily and their lands along the banks of the Holston River and there simply was no money to spare.

Sevier, however, had not given up and with Isaac Shelby, he approached John Adair, the land entry taker in North Carolina, who had just received 12,735 dollars in payments from the Scots-Irish settlers. Co Antrim-born Adair was a patriot sympathiser and a staunch Presbyterian and he did not need much persuasion to hand the money over as a loan to be used in recruiting the militia for the cause of independence.

With conviction, the intrepid Adair declared: "Colonel Sevier, I have no authority by law to make this disposition of the money. It belongs to the impoverished treasury of North Carolina and I dare not appropriate a cent of it to any purpose. But if the country is over-run by the British their liberty is gone. Take it, if the enemy, by its use, is driven from this country, I can trust that country to justify and vindicate my conduct. So take it".

Both Sevier and Shelby personally pledged to repay the money received from Adair after the War. It enabled the Overmountain men to be fully armed and prepared to face Colonel Patrick Ferguson and his loyalists at Kings Mountain.

The call to arms spread like wildfire through the North Carolina mountain and the Tennessee territory and on September 25, 1780 more than 1,000 would-be combatants gathered for enrolment on the low ground at Sycamore Shoals, which today is part of Elizabethton and near to Johnson City in East Tennessee.

Few of the men and boys musketing at Sycamore Shoals had the appearance of soldiers going into battle; they were small dirt farmers, who had just left their lands garbed in rough mountain-style clothes and carrying the barest of utensils. The most effective weapon each shouldered was the Kentucky long rifle, the traditional firepower of the 18th century American frontier.

Colonel John Sevier commanded 240 men from Washington county (then North Carolina now Tennessee!); Colonel Isaac Shelby led a similar force from nearby Sullivan county; Colonel William Campbell headed 400 Virginian riflemen and Colonel Charles McDowell commanded 160 from South Carolina. More joined from the Carolina Piedmont. By the time they reached Kings Mountain they numbered about 1,400, ranged against 1,100 under Patrick Ferguson.

The womenfolk and the children also gathered at Sycamore Shoals to bid their farewells and to ensure that the volunteers had enough food and clothing for the assignment. And present to offer spiritual guidance was the Presbyterian frontier pastor the Rev Samuel Doak, whose parents had emigrated from Co Antrim to the Shenandoah Valley of Virginia.

Doak, an old-style Presbyterian cleric in the best traditions of 18th century Calvinism, likened the cause of the patriot Overmountain settlers to that of Gideon and his people in opposing the Midianites in Old Testament Biblical times. The battle cry was "The Sword of the Lord and Gideon", with the assembled gathering loudly echoing Doak's words before starting off on horseback and foot to face Patrick Ferguson and the loyalists at Kings Mountain.

Virginian William Campbell, a six-foot six-inch giant of Ulster stock whose family had moved from Argyllshire in the 17th century Plantation years, was chosen as Overmountain men leader by Sevier, Shelby and McDowell and it took 10 days journeying before the patriot force got to within sight of Ferguson's Redcoat army.

Campbell's men dug into the wooded terrain, while Ferguson decided on an open base for his base. After reviewing the platoons under his command, William Campbell advised anyone who did not wish to fight to head for home immediately. There were no takers and after he ordered them to "shout like hell and fight like devils" his men, screaming at the top of their voices, responded to the first fire mounted from the loyalist ranks.

The battle of Kings Mountain lasted 65 minutes, with the patriot forces using Indian-style tactics to out-manoeuvre the loyalists from the back of virtually every tree, rock and shrub. There was much hand-to-hand fighting and the sharp shooting of the long riflemen took its toll.

The Redcoats were forced to defend their position with bayonets as the Overmountain men closed in. Colonel Ferguson, probably sensing defeat, had to personally head off attacks from all sides. A rifle shot struck him in the head and slumping in the saddle he dropped from his horse dead. His command was taken by Captain Abraham De-Peyster, who had engaged the Overmountain men in a previous battle at Musgrove's Mill.

The loyalists were hopelessly encircled and in panic some Redcoat soldiers waved white flags of surrender. But the shooting continued, with many of the patriots unaware of the significance of the white flags. They were not professional soldiers and the revenge factor surfaced as previous atrocities committed by loyalists came to mind.

Colonel Campbell managed to bring about a ceasefire among his ranks by calling out: "For God's sake, don't shoot. It is murder to kill them now, for they have raised their flags".

British officer De-Peyster protested at the behaviour of the patriots: "It's damned unfair, damned unfair".

Campbell calmly ignored the protestations, calling on the loyalists to sit down as prisoners. The Overmountain men had only minimal casualties compared to the loyalists: 28 killed and 62 wounded against 225 dead; 163 wounded and about 800 taken prisoner.

Kings Mountain was the watershed in the Revolutionary War, the left flank of Lord Cornwallis had been effectively shattered and the British were never again able to muster a loyalist force of size recruited from American society. Patrick Ferguson was buried close to the ridge he had chosen to defend.

Ferguson was just 36 when he died, a soldier whose bravery and technical military skills were as much admired by those whom he fought as those who had served under him.

Early in his American service, Patrick Ferguson wrote a letter to his mother which underlined his deep faith: "The length of our lives is not at our command, however much the manner of them may be. If our Creator enables us to act the part of honour and to conduct ourselves with spirit, probity and humanity, the change to another world whether now or in 50 years hence, will be for the worse".

The loyalist prisoners were taken to Hillsborough in North Carolina, where they were exchanged for patriot prisoners. Most of the Overmountain men drifted back to their farms and their families - their involvement in the War had ended.

A week elapsed before Lord Cornwallis learned of the news of the Kings Mountain defeat and it had a devastating effect. Plans for a major offensive on the southern and western frontier were abandoned although British authorities tried to dismiss the battle result as having no consequences.

General George Washington did not hear of the Kings Mountain battle until October 26, and, with elation, he spoke of "that important object gained" as "proof of the spirit and resources of the country".

In later years, United States President Thomas Jefferson was to recall "that memorable victory" at Kings Mountain - "the joyful annunciation of that turn of the tide of success which terminated the Revolutionary War with the seal of independence".

The Overmountain men militia officers at Kings Mountain became leading statesmen, politicians and civic leaders. John Sevier was the first Governor of Tennessee: Isaac Shelby the first Governor of Kentucky, while William Campbell represented Washington county in the Virginia House of Delegates before an untimely death 10 months after Kings Mountain. Many others were to distinguish themselves in politics, and in subsequent army careers, but most went back to being simple farmers.

Most of the Overmountain men (Wataugans) who fought at Kings Mountain were first, second and third generation Americans of Ulster-born parents or grandparents. A good many were born in

Ireland, the overwhelming number of them from Ulster, from the Presbyterian tradition.

Robert Leckie in his book George Washington's War said no breed of frontiersmen existed in America hardier than these settlements of mostly Scots-Irish along the Watauga and Holston River of North Carolina and the Tennessee territory.

"Fiercely independent, hunters, Indian fighters, deadly shots with those rifles, to which they gave names such as 'Sweet Lips' or 'Hot Lead', they could campaign for days on their horses with no other equipment than a blanket, a hunting knife and a bag of parched corn sweetened with molasses or honey," he wrote.

The Battle of Cowpens in South Carolina on January 17, 1781 involved quite a number of the Overmountainmen from Watauga and Scots-Irish settlers and militia soldiers of other ethnic groups from the Carolinas. The battle was another set-back for the British, with 1,000 patriot troops under the command of General Daniel Morgan routing the Redcoats under Colonel Banastre Tarleton.

British losses were more than 100 killed, more than 200 wounded and 600 captured. Militia casualties were 12 dead and 60 wounded and, as from Kings Mountain, support in the aftermath of Cowpens solidified support in the region for the American patriot cause and forced the British into desperate counter-manoeuvres.

Two months later, on March 15, 1781 at the battle of Guilford Courthouse in North Carolina, the British forces, although acknowledged to be victorious, lost more leeway in their desperate bid to hold on to the Carolinas. American casualties were less than 80 killed and 200 wounded, compared to nearly 100 killed and 400 wounded for the British.

The patriot militia retreated, while Lord Charles Cornwallis moved his exhausted Redcoat forces to Wilmington on the coast of North Carolina, effectively ceding the state to the enemy. The battle result and after-effects provoked radical English parliamentarian George Fox to declare in the House of Commons in London that "another such victory would destroy the British army".

Scots-Irish settlers, as at Kings Mountain and Cowpens, were also heavily involved in the fighting at Guilford Courthouse.

•••

The main thrust of the Rev Samuel Doak's sermon to the Overmountain militia men at Sycamore Shoals before they headed to Kings Mountain:

"My countrymen you are about to set out on an expedition which is full of hardships and dangers, but one in which the Almighty will attend you. The Mother Country has her hands upon you, these American colonies, and takes that for which our fathers planted their homes in the wilderness - OUR LIBERTY.

"Taxation without representation and the quartering of soldiers in the homes of our people without their consent are evidence that the Crown of England would take from its American subjects the last vestige of Freedom.

"Your brethren across the mountains are crying like Macedonia unto your help. God forbid that you shall refuse to hear and answer their call, but the call of your brethren is not all. The enemy is marching hither to destroy your homes.

"Brave men, you are not unacquainted with battle. Your hands have already been taught to war and your fingers to fight. You have wrested these beautiful valleys of the Holston and Watauga from the savage hand.

"Will you tarry now until the other enemy carries fire and sword to your very doors? No, it shall not be. Go forth then in the strength of your manhood to the aid of your brethren, the defence of your liberty and the protection of your homes. And may the God of justice be with you and give you victory.

"Let Us Pray: *Almighty and gracious God! Thou hast been the refuge and strength of Thy people in all ages. In time of sorest need we have learned to come to Thee - our Rock and our Fortress. Thou knowest the dangers and snares that surround us on march and in battle.*

"Thou knowest the dangers that constantly threaten the humble, but well beloved homes which Thy servants have left behind them.

"O, in Thine infinite mercy, save us from the cruel hand of the savage, and of tyrant. Save the unprotected homes while fathers and husbands and sons are far way fighting for freedom and helping the oppressed.

"Thou, who promised to protect the sparrow in its flight, keep ceaseless watch, by day and by night, over our loved ones. The helpless woman and little children, we commit to Thy care. Thou wilt not leave them or forsake them in times of loneliness and anxiety and terror.

"O God of battle, arise in Thy might. Avenge the slaughter of Thy people. Confound those who plot for our destruction. Crown this mighty effort with victory, and smite those who exalt themselves against liberty and justice and truth.

"Help us as good soldiers to wield the sword of the Lord and of Gideon. AMEN."

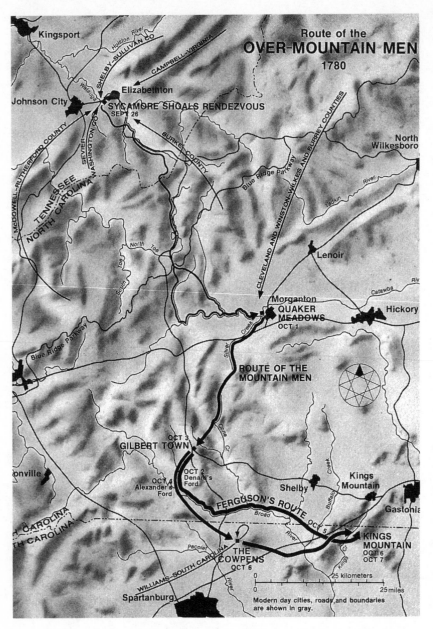

The route of the Scots-Irish Overmountain men to the Battle of Kings
Mountain, October 7, 1780.

23

George Bryan - *Presbyterian power-broker in Philadelphia during the War*

George Bryan, Pennsylvania's vice-president and acting president at the height of the Revolutionary War, was a Dublin-born Presbyterian who emigrated to America in 1752 as a 20-year-old and became a highly successful Philadelphia merchant and civic leader able to harness his ethnic-religious inheritance - Irish Presbyterianism.

Samuel Bryan, George's father, was a wealthy Dublin merchant who influenced a Philadelphia business associate James Wallace to enlist his son as a mercantile partner in a city that was literally teeming with Scots-Irish Presbyterian immigrants.

The Bryan and Wallace partnership lasted several years, before George Bryan found it more profitable to branch out as an independent merchant, trading between Philadelphia and England and Ireland in cotton and wool products and Irish linen, along with domestic goods such as a shears, needles, pins and buttons.

Bryan teamed up with Ulster merchants Redmond Conyngham (from Donegal!) and John Nesbitt to construct a 100-ton ship Hayfield, for transporting their imports across the Atlantic.

The Hayfield's first trek across the ocean took it to the Ulster port of Newry in Co Down in 1756 to participate in the flax seed trade. The ship returned eleven months later with a full cargo.

The Hayfield was headed back to Newry in December, 1757 to further the flax seed trade link, and on this voyage it also berthed at Dublin and Louisburg, Nova Scotia before returning to Pennsylvania.

Over a number of years the Hayfield made a number of successful trips across the Atlantic, travelling as far as Amsterdam in Holland, and, buoyed by the business that was flowing in his direction, George Bryan was by 1760 the owner of six vessels.

These were the years of the French and Indian War and the trade off-shoot from the hostilities were a bonus to Philadelphia merchants like Bryan. Gradually, he built up his fortune and diversified his investments by acquiring land property.

His most significant purchase was in 1761 when he bought more than 4,000 acres in Sussex and Morris counties in New Jersey from the London-based Pennsylvania land company for the then substantial sum of £2,750.

Like other men of his class, Bryan married into money, with his wife Elizabeth Smith, daughter of prominent Philadelphia Presbyterian merchant Samuel Smith. He not only married within his social status, but increased his contacts among the city's highly influential Presbyterian merchants.

Bryan's rise in the Pennsylvania business world was matched by a strengthening interest in Presbyterian church matters in the region and, from his election to the congregational committee of First Philadelphia in 1758, he became obligated as his father had advised him to "God and religion".

Presbyterianism in the American colonies at the time of George Bryan's involvement was undergoing dramatic changes, after the outpourings of the Great Awakening, inspired by English evangelist the Rev George Whitefield.

There was the New Side faction who argued that those who could testify to having been "saved" by God could be members of the church. Against this, the Old Side Presbyterians questioned the ability of revivalist ministers to pass judgment on an individual's alleged salvation.

The protracted New Side/Old Side debate lasted from 1742 to 1758, when the Articles of Union passed by the Synod of Philadelphia provided the basis for compromise.

George Bryan's First Philadelphia church was Old Side, while Second congregation in the city was New Side. Their rivalries extended beyond Calvinist theology, and was evident even in the business transactions between the main protagonists!

In church life in Pennsylvania, George Bryan had made his mark and, increasingly, he was looked upon by his peers as a man who could speak with authority for Presbyterian political interests.

Described by one church elder in 1766 as "our own hero", Bryan and his Presbyterian party had just reached a zenith in political influence in the state by removing the Quakers from the seat of power in Philadelphia.

George Bryan had been involved in dissenting politics since the mid-1750s, alongside Ulster-born Philadelphia teacher Charles Thomson. Initially, Bryan and his Scots-Irish Presbyterian co-religionists supported Benjamin Franklin and the Quaker establishment in the war against the Indians and in 1756, of the 24 elected officers in the city regiment, at least eight were Presbyterians.

However, as the hostilities continued with Indian attacks on isolated Scots-Irish settlements in the south-eastern and western parts of the province, tensions emerged and the relationship changed.

There was resentment at an alleged comment by Nathaniel Grubb, a Quaker party assemblymen, who, when informed in 1756 that several back-country frontiersmen had been murdered by Indians, remarked: "There are only some Scotch-Irish killed, who could well enough be spared.

Grubb denied the remark, but it added to the general feeling of mistrust between the Quakers and the Presbyterians, with the pacifism of the former at a time of great danger to life and limb an irritant to the hardy settlers from Ulster, who had one aim in view - of defeating the Indians.

The Quaker government in Philadelphia did not feel the need to built forts, establish militia or train scouts and Indian fighters.Their religious convictions and moral conscience demanded that they co-exist peacefully with the native Americans.

German settlers in Pennsylvania, particularly members of the Mennonnites, Moravians and the Amish sects, were also inclined, like the English Quakers, to retire rather than fight the Indians. Not so the Scots-Irish!

Some Presbyterian leaders, like Charles Thomson and Francis Allison, tried to keep relations cordial with Benjamin Franklin and the Quakers, but George Bryan by 1758 felt alienated from the Philadelphia assembly and decided that the best course was to campaign for its removal. He felt there had to be direct military confrontation with the Indians, stating: "We can expect no lasting peace, unless we bring the Indian enemy to reason."

Bryan's position, however, was not helped by violent vigilante activity by a group of about 50 Scots-Irish settlers from Paxton township at Conestoga and Lancaster in Lancaster county, who, in December 1763, avenged Indian killings of their people by putting to death 20 innocent Indians (men, women and children), some of them Christian converts.

The action of the "Paxton boys" in so irresponsibly and brutally taking the law into their own hands stunned and repulsed the Pennsylvania establishment and, with the approval of the Philadelphia assembly, Governor John Penn placed a substantial reward on the heads of the Paxton leaders and called for their capture and removal for trial.

The Scots-Irish settlers, however, were in no mood to be rebuked or threatened with the law over the killings. They remained defiant, arguing that their frontier settlements had been left largely unprotected in the pervading climate of war by their political masters among the pacifist Quaker fraternity in Philadelphia.

The settlers perceived that the government was supporting the Indians with funds which could have been used by them for adequate frontier defence against attack.

The Paxton group organised a march from Lancaster to Philadelphia to air their grievances before the Province's legislature, but before reaching the capital they were intercepted by four assemblymen led by Benjamin Franklin, who promised government relief if they returned home.

The Scots-Irish outlined the frontier grievances at length, with, significantly, the chief complaint inequality of backcountry settler representation in the Philadelphia assembly.

Governor Penn was still anxious to proceed with lawful proceedings against those responsible for the Conestoga and Lancaster murders, but the white settlers maintained it was improper to "deprive British subjects of their known privileges" if the trials were to take place outside the counties of residents of the defendants.

The matter dragged on, but the issues of properly administering justice to those guilty of the killings and ensuring proper defence for the white settlements were not effectively dealt with in the assembly debates which followed.

As a result, Governor Penn found it politically expedient to ignore the assembly demands for the immediate prosecution of the Paxton Boys and no one was ever charged for the killings.

The Paxton Boys insurrection placed George Bryan and his colleagues in a difficult position. Bryan, while unsympathetic to the Indians, was appalled by the Lancaster county massacre and alarmed by mob law. He reminded the Scots-Irish settlers of the "necessity of supporting order" and described the Paxton group as "mean and lower sort of people".

The Paxton group was also condemned by other leading Presbyterian dissenters in Philadelphia. However, in the cross-exchange that followed with George Bryan and others accusing the Quaker assembly members of sowing the seeds of the violence by their pacifism, pressing charges against those involved in the Paxton incident became less of a priority.

Relations worsened between the Presbyterians and the Quakers when Benjamin Franklin decided early in 1764 to petition the king-in-council to remove proprietor rule and bring the colony under royal government.

The Scots-Irish, victims of royal rule in the Scottish and Ulster homelands, completed vehemently opposed Franklin's strategy. In a petition circulated throughout the colony only 3,500 signatures favoured the transfer and 15,000 were against.

The scene was set for the bitterly fought assembly elections in October, 1764 and the Presbyterians forged alliances with the German Lutheran and Calvinist frontier communities and got surprise backing from some Anglican church leaders in Philadelphia.

George Bryan assumed a prominent role in the organisation of the Presbyterian vote in Pennsylvania, and he and former mayor Thomas Willing were selected for the task of ousting on a New Ticket platform the two most prominent Quaker politicians Benjamin Franklin and Joseph Galloway from the city's two seats.

Willing represented Philadelphia's wealthy and genteel society and was a leading importer of German immigrants, while Bryan appealed to the Calvinists, of Scots-Irish and German extraction.

The election was one of the most exciting and hotly contested in the history of Pennsylvania, with 3,900 voters participating in the county elections alone. By the narrowest of margins, Bryan and Willing defeated Franklin and Galloway, with eight of the 10 New Ticket candidates returned for the city and county of Philadelphia.

Overall in Pennsylvania, the Quakers still maintained a commanding majority, but their grip on power was loosening fast - the voice of the Scots-Irish was at last being listened to in the legislative corridors of Philadelphia.

George Bryan and his 10-strong minority group operated for a year in the assembly, but in the 1764 election their numbers were reduced to four and Bryan's political career went into decline. His financial affairs suffered a major set-back through a loss of trade and in 1771 he was declared bankrupt and also faced health problems.

The early 1770s were lean years for George Bryan, but in 1777 his political career shot back into prominence when he became a Philadelphia city assemblyman and was appointed Pennsylvania's vice-president and acting president. Bryan was one of the driving forces in the Pennsylvania government and under his leadership three aims were achieved: support of the state's war effort against the British, the subjugation of the state's Tories who opposed independence and the establishment of the state's revolutionary constitution.

George Bryan was not a member of the 1776 constitutional convention which drew up the Declaration of Independence, but he was a trusted aide of those who were involved.

Philadelphia in 1777 was in a state of chaos, after the upheaval from the signing of the Declaration and with the city's population fearful of attack from the British. Gradually, however, through the guidance of Bryan and others order was established by a Supreme Executive Council, which reorganised the courts and government departments.

For help in running the city, Bryan turned to two Presbyterian associates, including Declaration signer Thomas McKean, who took on the chief justice's role. The assistant justice post went to John Evans and attorney-general to John Dickinson.

Later, London-trained lawyer and leading Philadelphia Presbyterian Joseph Reed assumed the presidency with Bryan as his deputy. Reed's grandfather had emigrated from Carrickfergus in Co Antrim.

Other senior civil and military appointments were made from within the Presbyterian fold in Pennsylvania, men who George Bryan obviously felt he could trust at a time of great uncertainty and instability.

After decades of being subservient to Quaker rule, the Scots-Irish Presbyterians from the city and backcountry were now calling the shots in Philadelphia under the banner of the Constitutional Party.

By 1780, George Bryan and his friends were at the pinnacle of their power, keeping Presbyterian interests foremost among their concerns.

Their influence continued right through the War years, certainly until 1789 when Londonderry-born Charles Thomson was authorised by the Continental Congress to travel to Mount Vernon in Virginia to tell George Washington that it was the wish of Congress that he become the first President of the United States.

The Scots-Irish were the main players in the many facets of life in the new nation that was unfolding.

"It is the most remarkable and singular coincidence that the constitution of the Presbyterian Church should bear such a close and striking resemblance to the political constitution of our country."

The Hon. WILLIAM C. PRESTON,
South Carolina.

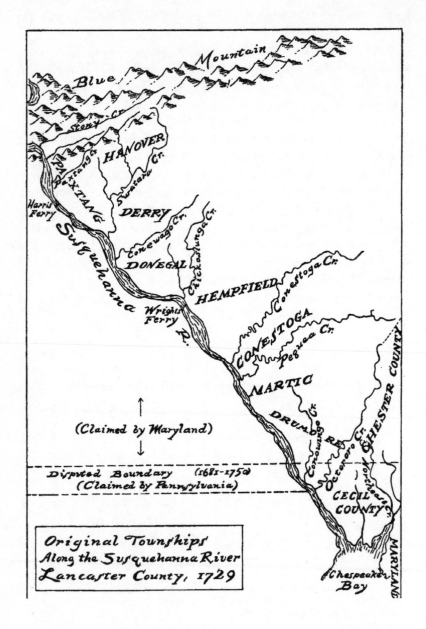

Eastern Pennsylvania where the Scots-Irish have been an influential community since the early 18th century.

24

Rev. Francis Allison - *favoured preacher to the Continental Congress*

Ulster Presbyterian minister and teacher the Rev Francis Allison played a key role in shaping opinions on American independence from the mother country and his pupils included three of the most eminent members of the Continental Congress in Philadelphia - Thomas McKean, Charles Thomson and George Read.

Francis Allison, born at Leck near Letterkenny, Co Donegal in 1704, studied for several years under leading Ulster academic Francis Hutchinson at Glasgow University, and emigrated to America in 1735.

Hutchinson, from Saintfield in Co Down, had spent some time in Dublin in the company of radical thinkers Jonathan Swift, William King, Robert Molesworth and Thomas Rundle, and, when he moved to Glasgow University in 1730, he became a founder of what was then known as the Scottish "Enlightenment" and of a liberalised Presbyterianism.

Allison, a leading advocate of the Old Side Presbyterian faction which split with a more evangelical New Side group in the American colonies during the 1742-58 period, opened an academy in Philadelphia in 1743.

The academy was recognised by the Presbyterian Synod and was later moved to Newark, Delaware, becoming the foremost college outside of New York.

In 1752, Allison returned to Philadelphia to convert the Latin School to the degree-awarding College of Philadelphia and for the next three decades his educational influence was marked on those who were to play a key role in the Revolution.

Benjamin Franklin, never one to espouse too readily the Scots-Irish, held Allison as a man of "great ingenuity and learning", even despite his Calvinist theological orthodoxy.

Echoing much of what he learned under the tutorship of Francis Hutcheson, Allison conveyed in blunt Ulster tones: "The end of all civil power is the public happiness and any power not conducive to this is unjust and the people who gave it may justly abolish it."

During the War years, Francis Allison preached to the Continental Congress. Hardly surprising, considering his former pupils included Thomson, McKean and Read, who, when students in secondary and collegiate courses, actually lived in their master's house.

Allison taught almost every subject and it was said that his influence outlasted any distance he created in his students. Historians agree that it is not an exaggeration to say that Allison's view coloured the whole definition of the clamour of the break with Britain in Pennsylvania.

A precursor to the Thomas Jefferson authorised version of the Declaration of Independence was a document compiled in June, 1776 by the Pennsylvania revolutionary committee, under Thomas McKean's direction.

Its wording was virtually a duplicate of the philosophy of the Presbyterian mentors Francis Hutcheson and Francis Allison: "Whereas George the Third . . in violation of the principles of the British constitution, and of the laws, justice and humanity, hath by an accumulation of oppression excluded the inhabitants of this, with other colonies, from his protection, and whereas, the obligations of allegiance (being reciprocal between a king and his subjects!), are now dissolved".

25

Boyd's Creek - *only Revolutionary War battle on Tennessee soil*

The only engagement of the Revolutionary War to be fought within the boundaries of the existing state of Tennessee was the battle of Boyd's Creek in Sevier county in the heart of the Great Smoky Mountains on December 16, 1780. Then, a consignment of East Tennessee militia riflemen, led by Colonel John Sevier, defeated a large force of Chickamauga Cherokee and renegade Indians, who were operating in support of the British.

The Cherokee tribes had earlier attacked the Watauga Scot-Irish settlements along the Holston and French Broad rivers while Colonel Sevier and his Overmountain men were away fighting at the battle of Kings Mountain and at Boyd's Creek the Indians suffered heavy casualties.

Early in 1780, the Chickamauga Cherokees, led by their militant chief Dragging Canoe, were persuaded by British agents to begin attacking the frontier settlements in the south east and this squalid agreement became more important to colonial commander Lord Charles Cornwallis after the defeat of Colonel Patrick Ferguson's force at the battle of Kings Mountain.

Sensing weakness of the Watauga settlements while their men were still in South Carolina at Kings Mountain, senior British officer Colonel Thomas Brown sent one of his agents to Dragging Canoe and little encouragement was needed to send the Chickamaugas on the march north.

They passed through the Overhill Cherokee towns and, on the way, Dragging Canoe recruited more warriors to follow him. However, a few Cherokees were unhappy with the plan to attack the frontier settlements and Nancy Ward, who had connections to both the white and native American races and was known on the frontier as the "beloved woman of the Cherokees", sent two traders - Isaac Thomas and Ellis Harlan - to alert the Watauga people of the danger.

On arrival back from Kings Mountain, John Sevier learned of Dragging Canoe's intentions and almost immediately he marched southwards with several hundred men, intent on halting the Indians before they forded the French Broad River.

Sevier and his men confronted a small band of Indians on December 15 and, after driving them off, they pressed on, crossing the French Broad River and camping at Boyd's Creek.

On the morning of December 16, their scouts discovered the main Indian camp about three miles away and as Sevier's men approached, they found the Cherokees stalked out in a half-moon formation, planning an ambush.

A small group of Overmountain men attacked the Indian lines, while the main body feigned a retreat to lure the Indians into a trap. As a number of Indian warriors fell, Dragging Canoe and others retreated into a nearby swamp away from the battle field.

The engagement did not last long, the Cherokee threat to the Watauga settlements had ended with Dragging Canoe and his surviving warriors fleeing the region. Minimal casualties were reported on the patriot side, but more than 30 Indians were killed.

Within a few days, Colonel John Sevier was joined by the Kings Mountain patriot commander Colonel William Campbell and his aide Major Joseph Martin and, as the entire Overmountain force headed south, they burned several Cherokee towns in retaliation.

Boyd's Creek in Sevier county is close to Dumpling Creek, where, on June 10, 1785 a treaty was conducted between the white settlers led by John Sevier, David Kennedy, Ebenezer Alexander and the Cherokee Indians, led by "King" Ancoo of Chota.

This treaty authorised that all of Jefferson, Hamblen, Sevier, Knox and Blount counties, in what was to become 11 years later part of the new state of Tennessee, be opened up to settler homesteads.

The treaty outlined that "liberal compensation" be made to the Cherokees for the land that had been ceded and granted by them to the white people on the south side of the Holston and French Broad rivers to the region of the Tennessee river close to Knoxville. Within three years more than 1,000 families, most of them of Scots-Irish origin, had moved in and established homesteads on these historic Indians lands.

It was very dangerous territory for the early white settlers and, as a means of protection and communal vantage point, they established fort stations or blockhouses. The McGaughey, McTeer, McCroskey, Hunter and Houston forts on the trail between Sevierville and Knoxville acted as safe havens for the various families.

The McFarlands were a typical Scots-Irish Presbyterian family on the North Carolina/Tennessee frontier during the Revolutionary War and several generations fought with distinction on the patriot side. The McFarlands, who had moved through the Shenandoah Valley of Virginia, settled at Hamblen county in north east Tennessee, the region known as the "Irish Bottom" due to the preponderance of Scots-Irish settlers there.

Colonel Robert McFarland, a militia leader in the War, followed in the soldiering tradition of his father Robert, who fought at the Battle of Mount Pleasant in 1774. Robert Sen. and his father John and other members of the family had emigrated from Co Antrim about 1746 and settled first at Augusta county in the Shenandoah, where he became a local church elder and a militia lieutenant.

Born in Virginia, Colonel Robert McFarland entered military service in 1776. He served through the Revolutionary War in various battles on the frontier region and took part in the Colonel Arthur Campbell-led campaign against the Cherokee towns of Chota, Chilhowee, Little Tellico and Chestowah in December 1780 after the aborted attack on the Watauga settlements by Dragging Canoe and the tribes.

A son of Colonel McFarland, also named Robert, was commended for his heroism at the War of 1812 in the battle of Lundy Lane in upper Canada, while his son, another Robert, led the 31st/39th Tennessee Mounted Infantry at the Civil War battle of the Piedmont in Staunton, Virginia on June 6, 1864.

The scene at Sycamore Shoals on September 25, 1780 where the Scots-Irish Overmountain men gathered before heading to the Battle of Kings Mountain. Picture by Lloyd Branson.

26

Dissenting zeal *of Rev. William Martin*

Many Ulster Presbyterian clerics created an unfavourable impression with British colonial interests in America at the time of the Revolutionary War. They were seen as "turbulant priests", unwilling to conform or move their congregations away from the dissenting path that was leading to independence from the Crown.

Covenanting pastor the Rev William Martin was a thorn in the flesh of the British authorities in his South Carolina Piedmont parish and so strong was the revolutionary tone of his sermons to his people that he was arrested and his church burned down by British forces.

Martin, a Presbyterian of the Reformed code, was born at Ballyspollum near Ballykelly in Co Londonderry in 1729 and, when minister of the church at Ballymoney in Co Antrim, his uncompromising advocacy of the gospel was matched by his fearless outspokenness against the Anglican Church - influenced British authorities who had been discriminating against the Ulster Presbyterians on the matter of religious and civil rights.

After a sustained period of excessive rent demands and eviction of tenants from their homesteads in rural parts of Ulster like Ballymoney, William Martin declared from his pulpit that "enough was enough".

"Anyone who knows anything about the Ulster countryside realises that the rents are so high that the land does not bring in enough to pay them. Many of us are beggared and in time all would be," he told his congregation in 1772, adding that as a minister he could not stand idly by and await the violence and ruin that would come.

"Steps should be taken now to see that such situations did not develop," Martin advised and he suggested that they all pool their limited resources and send to Belfast to charter ships for emigration to South Carolina, where they would "obtain free land and live free men."

With other Covenanting families, the Rev William Martin and his congregation left for Charleston in five ships during the autumn of 1772 - the James and Mary and Lord Dunluce sailing from Larne; the Pennsylvania Farmer and the Hopewell from Belfast and the Free Mason from Newry. In all 467 families, representing more than 1,000 people, set sail.

Many Ulster immigrants arrived in South Carolina under the "bounty" scheme. This entitlement of £4 was being offered to "poor Protestants" from Europe to settle in the region, with small amounts paid to children. The Scots-Irish took advantage of the bounty and when the offer was abolished in 1768 the South Carolina authorities ruled that the settlers should be given the lands free.

William Martin and his Ballymoney congregation settled on the free Carolina lands, alongside Seceders, a splinter Presbyterian group from neighbouring Ballyrashane, Derrykeghan and Kilraughts in North Antrim.

They initially combined in a Reformed union church at Rocky Mountain Road, about 15 miles from the South Carolina town of Chester, appropriately called "Catholic", but later Martin moved to their own log church two miles further along.

The Revolutionary War had just broken out and it provided William Martin with the opportunity to remind his congregation of why they had to leave their Ulster homeland and he bluntly denounced the British colonial rulers.

Recalling the hardships their fathers had endured in religion and in their possessions, Martin pointed out: "They had been forced out of Ireland, had come over to America and cleared their lands and homes and their church and were free men."

Martin warned that the British were coming into the region and soldiers would again be depriving them of the fruits of their labours and would be driving them out. They should not stand, he said, meekly and idly by while all they had wrought was taken from them.

"There was a time to pray and a time to fight and the time to fight had come," he implored.

Two companies of militiamen were formed from the congregation and the next day they set off with arms and horses to join the American revolutionary army. Martin's sermon, had ominously reached the ears of British commanders in the region and soon his church was burned down.

Martin was even brought before Lord Charles Cornwallis to give an account of his activities, such was in his reputation with the British. When he was released, he lived for a period in the strong Presbyterian dissenting community of Mecklenburg county in North Carolina, but after the British surrender at Yorktown he returned to Chester county and resumed charge of his congregation.

The Revolutionary War service of William Martin and 64 of his congregation from the Catholic Presbyterian Church at Chester county, South Carolina is recorded in a memorial at the church, unveiled in 1933. Almost all were first generation Ulster-Scots.

It was common for most of the male members of Presbyterian congregations in the backwoods territories to join the militia units involved in the independence struggle. Historical acounts of the Nazareth congregation in another part of the South Carolina Piedmont show that every ablebodied man fought for the patriot cause.

They were at the battles of Kings Mountain, Cowpens, Charleston, Yorktown, Valley Forge, and Ninety Six, significant encounters on the frontier. Between battles, these farmers were allowed to return to their homes for the protection of their families against Indian attack, and when they were needed, the word was spread quickly from neighbour to neighbour.

The Nazareth Presbyterians formed the Spartan regiment, from which the town of Spartanburg gots its name, and it was said their womenfolk showed "as much fortitude in suffering and hardship as the men displayed in fighting".

Staking for Religious Freedom

Scots-Irish Presbyterians made a significant contribution to the campaign for religious freedom in America during the 18th century.

Prior to the Declaration of Independence all persons, even dissenters, were required to pay contributions to the Established Church. But the Declaration of Independence made this seem incongruous so that many ministers were in a quandary what to do.

At the first meeting of the Hanover Presbytery in Virginia after the adoption of the Declaration of Independence, a memorial to the legislature of Virginia was prepared setting out cogent reasons for complete separation of church and state.

This memorial closed with the following appeal:

"Therefore we ask no ecclesiastical establishments for ourselves: neither can we approve of them when granted to others. This indeed would be giving exclusive or separate emoluments or privileges to one set of men, without any special public services, to the common reproach and injury of every other denomination."

After a bitter debate in which Thomas Jefferson supported the Presbyterian memorialists the law for separation was passed on December 5, 1776.
Separation was advocated not by those who desired to destroy religion but by the Presbyterians, the Baptists and the Quakers. There was no intention to weaken religion but to make it a matter of free choice.

27

Hardy frontierswomen who became
real heroines of the War

Scots-Irish womenfolk of the Appalachian backcountry
performed significant heroics during the Revolutionary War and
many went beyond their normal call of domestic duty in the
home to ensure that their husbands, sons and brothers in the American
patriot militia units received all the back-up they needed in resources.

Margaret Catherine (Kate) Barry, from Walnut Grove, Spartanburg
in South Carolina, is considered one of the outstanding heroines of the
Revolutionary War, for the part she played in saving lives during the
Battle of Cowpens in January 1781.

Another heroine was Mary McKeehan Patton, who, with her
Ulster-born husband John Patton, made the gunpowder that was used
by the Overmountain Men from the Watauga region of North Carolina
at the Battle of Kings Mountain.

Kate Barry was the daughter of Co Antrim couple Charles and
Mary Barry Moore, who emigrated to America and about 1750. She
was a woman of hardy resolve, married at 15 to Captain Andrew
Barry, who was also from a Scots-Irish family that had settled in the
Tyger River region of South Carolina.

Andrew Barry was a captain of the South Carolina Rangers during
the War and he commanded militia companies at the battles of
Fishing Creek, Musgrove's Mill (where he was wounded!) and at
Cowpens.

The couple had eleven children, five sons and six daughters, and
Kate performed duties as a volunteer scout and guide for the South

Carolina Piedmont patriots, always acting in support of her husband. Her scouting operations centred mainly in Spartanburg county and, being an excellent horsewoman, she was able to cover the thick wooded terrain and Indian trails with speed of movement.

Kate frequently rode to where the patriots were camped to warn of impending danger and, with the help of a black slave Uncle Cato, she completed many successful scouting operations. Hollow trees would be filled with corn to provide against food shortages. Very often, after raids by British forces, settler homes were left destitute and the corn caches in the trees were used to feed the people and the animals.

This highly motivated frontierswoman even engaged in rounding up militia troops when reinforcements were required. At the battle of Cowpens she took responsibility for gathering up patriot groups and moving them to strategic points in the frontline of battle.

Her husband was holding the line with General Andrew Pickens against the British Redcoat troops under the command of Banastre Tarleton, a Merseysider from the north of England, who was a much reviled figure in the Scots-Irish communities of Charlotte and the Waxhaws.

As the battle ensured at Cowpens, the women of Nazarath Presbyterian Church, 13 miles away, were assembled in a house near the church and a vigilant Kate Barry was at the shoals on the Tyger River, waiting for reports from the battlefield.

When news of the crushing victory for the patriots was passed along she rushed to the Church to inform the women. At Cowpens, 926 of Tarleton's troops were killed, captured or wounded and many armaments were taken. On the American side, 132 were killed and 60 wounded.

On another occasion when the British, led by "Bloody Bill" Cunningham, made an infamous raid into the area, Kate heard them across the river near her father's home at Walnut Grove. She tied her two-year-old daughter Catherine (Little Katie) to a bed post for safety and rode to her husband's company for help. Her action forced the British to retreat.

Once, when the Redcoats came to Kate's home demanding to know the whereabouts of Andrew Barry's company, she refused to co-operate and was tied up and struck three times with a leash. This attack angered the men of her husband's company, for it was said any one of them would have given his own life to save hers.

Again, on a separate front, with the British in hot pursuit, Kate swam her horse across the Pacolet River near Hurricane Shoals. Fortunately, the water rose to a high level just as Kate and the horse reached dry ground on the other side, thus preventing the British from capturing her and the important message that she carried.

The heroic deeds of Kate Barry have been part of South Carolina folklore for more than 200 years and today her memory is revered by many people of of the Spartanburg and Greenville areas.

Kate's nephew was Senator William Taylor Barry, who was President Andrew Jackson's Postmaster General in the White House, after soldiering with Jackson in the War of 1812-13. He was also United States minister to Spain.

Mary Patton, the powder maker, learned the art from her Scottish father David when they lived in England and she married Ulster Presbyterian John Patton in 1772 after their families settled in eastern Pennsylvania.

The Pattons headed down the Shenandoah Valley with their two children and made a home at Sycamore Shoals- Elizabethton in North Carolina. There, along with Andrew Taylor, another Scots-Irish settler, the Pattons established a gunpowder mill for serving to the local militia.

Mary was the real expert in the manufacture of powder, simply made with the use of a large black kettle. She was able to supply 500 pounds of black gunpowder for use by the Overmountain Men from the Sycamore Shoals area for the Battle at Kings Mountain on October 9, 1780.

The gunpowder was a highly potent mix which proved very effective for the long rifles the patriot militias used. The processes of manufacture of black gunpowder were the production of saltpeter and charcoal and in the cottage industry of the operation in the Patton household mill, much hand labour was necessary. The powder was packed in 25, 50 and 100 pound kegs.

The contribution which Mary Patton and her husband John made to the Revolutionary War effort may not have made the national headlines, but in North Carolina and East Tennessee their names figure prominently in the annals.

Three Pattons - Robert, Thomas and Matthew, all from a Scots-Irish background, are listed as having fought in the Battle of Kings Mountain. Matthew Patton was also listed at Cowpens.

Mary taught other members of her family to manufacture gunpowder and the Patton mill continued in production in East Tennessee for close on 100 years. It was used by the Confederate Army during the Civil War.

Firing a Musket

Musket balls used by militia soldiers in the American Revolutionary War were made from lead melted in a crucible and then poured into a mould. Once the ball had cooled, it was removed, and the excess lead, or "spruce", was clipped away.

The powder necessary for a single shot could be measured and charged by hand. However, with instant action required in battle, soldiers improvised by using paper cartridges containing a ball and a premeasured charge of powder.

With the firelock at half cock, a small amount of powder was fired into the pan as a primer. The remaining powder was emptied down the muzzle, followed by the ball together with the cartridge paper, which held the ball in place. The rammer forced the entire package down the muzzle.

Rifles were fired differently depending on their range. Musket barrels were smooth and larger in diameter than the balls they fired, which made them easy to load. For greater accuracy, rifle barrels were grooved to spin each ball, so it had to fit tightly.

A piece of cloth called a patch was used to make the fit snug and it was rammed down with the ball, then trimmed.

- A -

28

Contrasting view from Ireland
on the Revolutionary War

D uring the American Revolutionary War, Sir John de Blacquire
presented, on behalf of Roman Catholics in Ireland, an address
to King George 111 in London "abhorring the unnatural
rebellion which has lately broken out among some of his American
subjects".

This may seem odd to many in the Ireland of today for it is somewhat of a paradox that generally Irish Protestant and Roman Catholic
attitudes to Britain during the American Revolutionary War were so
different from what currently prevails, with almost all the Protestants
(unionists) now backing the maintenance of the Union and the
overwhelming majority of Roman Catholics (nationalist) seeking
separation and the setting up of an all-Ireland republic.

Interestingly, a large swathe of middle class Roman Catholic
opinion in Ireland, in both the clerical and lay sectors, publicly
supported the British war effort in America in the 1770s.

It was the view of many leading Irish Roman Catholics that the
best way to undermine the penal laws which were in vogue against
them at the time was to demonstrate that they were more loyal to the
Crown than Protestants.

When the War broke out in 1775, a group of influential Roman
Catholics in Dublin sent memorials to the British authorities, stating
their abhorrence of the Presbyterian rebellion in America and offering
to encourage recruitment, even though Roman Catholic enlistment at
the time was barred. This group described the American Revolution as
an "unnatural rebellion".

In Limerick, Roman Catholic leaders, both clergy and laity, raised half a guinea per volunteer for the first two hundred men to enlist in the British army. In the Co Down town of Newry, Roman Catholic merchants publicly aligned themselves with British interests in quelling the Presbyterian uprising in America. Loyal addresses were also sent to London from Cork, an overwhelmingly Roman Catholic city.

This attitude by Irish Roman Catholics was entirely in line with that taken by the Vatican, where the then Pope in 1760 gave full recognition to British monarch King George 111, a high-church Anglican, on the King's assension to the Throne.

The fall-out from the aborted Roman Catholic-supported rebellions against the Crown in Scotland in 1715 and 1745 had run its course and both the Irish and Scottish Church hierarchies were broadly on track with the established order in the British Isles.

In return for their support in the American War, the British government provided legal relief for the Roman Catholics in Ireland and Scotland, legislation which effectively freed the Roman Catholics from educational, marital and professional disabilities.

Anglicans or members of the Church of Ireland, many of whom held civil positions under the Crown in the administration run from Dublin Castle, were also generally agreeable to the continuance of British interests in the American colonies.

However, in these Irish cities and towns there was a significant measure of Protestant Whig support for the American revolution, as was evidenced by referenda conducted among its citizens. Roman Catholics were disenfranchised at the time.

Of course, most of the American revolutionaries, their religion shaped by a radical dissenting form of Protestantism, were not sympathetic to the hierarchal systems of the Anglican and Roman Catholic churches. Indeed, there was an innate suspicion by some of the Revolutionary leaders of the Roman Catholic Church and its monolithic all-pervading traditions.

Some historians claim a major context of the American Revolution was Protestant colonialist fear over the Quebec Act of 1774 which recognised Roman Catholicism in the Canadian Province and extended Quebec territory to the Ohio River. There was also Protestant colonial concern among Presbyterians and Congregationalists that Anglican Bishops might be appointed from England to North America.

Ulster Presbyterians were warmly sympathetic with the fight for independence on the other side of the Atlantic, not surprising since their kinsmen who had emigrated in large numbers over a period of half a century were in the vanguard of the struggle in Pennsylvania and the Appalachian frontier backcountry.

In 1775, two hundred and fifty leading citizens of Belfast, almost to a man Presbyterian, called on King George 111 in London to "dismiss his Ministers and sheath his sword".

Historian George Bancroft observed Protestant attitudes in the north of Ireland to fight across the Atlantic: "The Oakboys and the Hearts of Steel with their other relatives were being well and favourably heard from in George Washington's army, and Ulster's sympathy and best wishes were with them and the cause they were fighting."

At the end the War in 1783, the Presbyterian-influenced Yankee Club of Stewartstown in Co Tyrone sent a message of congratulations to George Washington at his Mount Vernon home in Virginia. Washington acknowledged the Stewartstown message with appreciative sentiments.

Armagh Presbyterian minister the Rev Dr William Campbell, as Moderator of the Synod of Ulster in the 1770s/1780s, said the Presbyterians of Ulster condemned the American War of Independence as "unjust, cruel and detestable".

Newry-born Campbell, minister of First Armagh congregation and chaplain to Lord Charlemont's regiment of volunteers in Ulster, declared: "The Presbyterians of Ulster beheld the War with anguish and with horror, as the most wanton, unprovoked despotism.

"Their friends and relations abounded in the different provinces of America, and they heard with pride that they composed the flower of Washington's army, being carried on by a native love of liberty, to encounter every danger for the safety of their adopted country."

W. E. Lecky, late 19th century author of The American Revolution (1763-1783), wrote: "Protestant Ireland (in 1776) was indeed far more earnestly enlisted on the side of the Americans than any other portion of the Empire. Emigrants from Ulster formed a great part of the American army, and the constitutional question of the independence of the Irish Parliament was closely connected with the American question.

"The movement of opinion, however, was confined to Protestants, The Catholic gentry on this, as on all other questions of national danger, presented addresses to the King attesting in strong terms their loyalty."

Recruitment to the British Army for service in America during the Revolutionary War brought resistance in some Presbyterian strongholds of Ulster with many unwilling to fight their co-religionists in the far-off colonies.

One such area of discontent was Strabane in Co Tyrone, where a large section of the 5,000-strong population were of Scottish Planter stock, kin to those who had sailed from Londonderry to the American colonies through the 18th century.

Quite apart from the human trail across the Atlantic, Strabane had strong links with America with the linen industry benefiting from flaxseed imports from Philadelphia, through the enterprise of local man Samuel Carson, who had become a leading merchant in the Pennsylvania capital.

•••

• Strabane was the home town of John Dunlap, printer of the Declaration of Independence, and of James Wilson, the grandfather of President Woodrow Wilson. James Wilson emigrated from Londonderry to Pennsylvania in 1807.

29

Loyalist families *among the Scots-Irish*

While the Scots-Irish Presbyterians gained a high profile for declaring for the patriot cause in the American War of Independence, a significant number remained loyal to the Crown, particularly in the Carolina backcountry.

The dividing lines were not so clear in some areas of the Carolinas with instances of frontier militia men changing sides more than once over the duration of War. Members of the same family fought on opposite sides in the War, with father pitted against son; brother against brother and neighbour against neighbour with hostilities on some fronts taking on the mantra of a civil war.

The Scots-Irish, whether patriot or loyalist, could easily identify the native American tribes as their enemy, but it was much more difficult to come to terms with fighting men from their own ethnic immigrant strain.

It is generally reckoned that more than three-quarters of the Scots-Irish settlers were sympathetic in varying degrees to the clamour for American independence, but those who fought for the Crown and the maintenance of the link with Britain were not an inconsiderable number. Indeed, some historians estimate there were as many as 25,000 Carolina loyalists who bore arms against the American patriots.

Support for loyalism (or Toryism!) was ironically strongest in areas of the Carolinas where the Regulation movements had operated in the years leading up the War. Regulators - local vigilantes - were pledged to take action, even outside the law, against exorbitant taxes and fees set by landlords and officials acting on behalf of the colonial authorities.

The Scots-Irish outnumbered the other ethnic strains in the militant Regulation movements, but English and German backcountry farmers also participated, and by the late 1760s up to eight Carolina backcountry countries were in Regulatory control.

The Regulatory activities lasted about five years and in 1771 things came to a head in bloody exchanges at Alamance in North Carolina where Irish-born Governor William Tryon broke up the movement. A number of Regulators were hanged by the provincial authorities for serious crimes committed.

The South Carolina Regulators may have violently railed against the colonial establishment in the years before the War, but by 1775 they would have been considered half-hearted patriots. The hostilities provided Regulators and ex-Regulators, who had secured forgiveness for their past illegal actions by taking the oath of loyalty to the Crown, with the opportunity of paying off old sores.

All around them in the Carolina backcountry the Regulators found their former enemies in control of government affairs and the view was taken that it was better to remain under British colonial rule than change to a government run by easterners from the gentry class, albeit from the Scots-Irish diaspora, who had never shown any sympathy for them, and effectively suppressed their movement.

The Continental Congress, aware of the dissenting voices in the Carolinas against their independence call, sent two Presbyterian ministers to North Carolina, at a salary of forty dollars a month, to try to win backing for the patriot cause.

Joseph Hewes and William Hooper, North Carolina delegates to the Continental Congress, persuaded Presbyterian ministers in Pennsylvania to write to fellow church members in the Carolinas to persuade them on the merits of the revolution.

But, set against the strong patriotic feelings in Mecklenburg and the Waxhaws areas, this call resulted in at best only lukewarm support in other parts of the Carolinas backcountry.

Alexander Chesney, who was born in Dunclug near Ballymena in Co Antrim in 1756, is probably the best known of the Scots-Irish loyalists in the Carolina Piedmont and it is remarkable that when the

War ended in 1782 he returned home to spend the last years of his life in Ulster.

Interestingly, Chesney and a local Scots-Irish compatriot Moses Kirkland in the Carolina backcountry, bore arms against the Crown in situations where they were compelled to, but tactically switched sides when the opportunity arose.

Chesney's father was Robert McChesney - the "Mc" was dropped when the family moved to Charleston in 1772 - and they were given 100 acres of land on backcountry territory reserved for incoming Irish Protestant settlers. The Chesneys were aligned with the Ulster immigrant families of Purdy, Gillespey, Archbold, Wilson, Symonton, Cook, Nisbit, Grier, Wylie, McCleland, Barclay, Pogue, Phillips and Brandon and their influence extended widely in the frontier settlements.

The Chesneys were only a few years on the Carolina frontier when hostilities commenced and the agitation for independence began to be felt. The backcountry Scots-Irish settlers were isolated from the political wrangling that took place in Pennsylvania and Virginia, and Charleston, but the seeds of dissension were still being sown and the clamour for independence was heard more stridently.

Alexander Chesney, Moses Kirkland, John Philips, Joshua English and Andrew Williamson were men who were exerting a large degree of influence on the Scots-Irish families in the Carolina backcountry townships of Belfast, Londonderry (Londonborough) and Williamburg.

However, when attempts were made in July, 1775 by the revolutionary council to persuade the frontier settlers to sign a document refusing to import or buy British goods and withholding an allegiance to the Crown - Chesney, Kirkland, Philips and the others resolved not to get involved.

Alexander Chesney and his neighbours chose instead to remain faithful to King George 111, who they perceived as being a benevolent benefactor, and they organised themselves into defence groups.

In November, 1775 these South Carolina backcountry loyalists engaged in the first military battle with the patriot militia - at Ninety Six, where, after emerging victorious, they dispersed on learning that a superior force was on its way from the coastal areas.

Alexander Chesney led many of the loyalists to his father's lands and they hid in caves until the danger was averted. The loyalist faction among the Scots-Irish settlers joined on the side of the Redcoat army under Patrick Ferguson at Kings Mountain and Banastre Tarleton at Cowpens.

Among those of Scots-Irish vintage who fought under Chesney were John Adams, William Atkins, Charles Brandon, Christopher Brandon, Robert Chesney (father), William Chesney (brother), William Cunningham, Hugh Cook, Jonathan Frost, Matthew Gillespey, John Heron (brother-in-law), Robert McWhorter and James Millar.

Alexander Chesney was captured several times by the patriots, once after the battle of King Mountain.

When the War ended, some of the Scot-Irish loyalists evacuated with the British from Charleston in December, 1782. They went first to Florida or islands in the Caribbean and from there to Nova Scotia. Others went to England, or like, Alexander Chesney returned directly to Ireland.

They settled chiefly in Belfast, Larne, Ballymena, Lisburn and Bangor and obtained posts with the British government mainly in customs. Chesney was given a civil service appointment in Bangor, Co. Down, an area with a strong Presbyterian presence.

The majority, however, of the Scots-Irish loyalists chose to remain in South Carolina and returned to their homes and land on the frontier. There, provided they had not committed what were regarded as war crimes against their fellow South Carolinans, they were permitted to melt back into society.

Some were imprisoned, a number were burnt out of their homes, but a large number managed to satisfactorily mend fences with their neighbours and were able to live together thereafter in harmony.

•••

• Alexander Chesney left behind a very detailed account of his experiences on the loyalist side in the Revolutionary War, and his original diary is preserved for posterity in the Northern Ireland Public Records Office in Belfast.

Scots-Irish in opposition to the Revolution

During the struggle for independence by the Scots-Irish along the American frontier in the 1770s/1780s, there were some who publicly declared their opposition to the break with the mother country, and the old order. These people were labelled Tories or loyalists or just   disaffected persons.

One such person was Ulster Presbyterian minister the Rev Alexander Miller, who moved to a congregation in Augusta county in the Shenandoah valley of Virginia in October, 1775 just as the war was beginning. Miller accused members of the Augusta county patriot committee in Staunton of being "seditious persons and traitors", which led to his shunning by many in this patriotic Scots-Irish community.

Miller persisted in his public opposition, arguing that the Revolution was wrong in that it deprived Great Britain of "her rightful property", and, because of the evils which emerged out of it: trade was stopped, taxes were increased and oaths of allegiance were violated.

The outspoken cleric was hauled before the Augusta court where he was found guilty of endeavouring by "words and sentences" to "support, maintain and defend the power and authority" of the "King of Great Britain". He was placed under heavy bond and confined to his estate for the duration of the war. Two months later Miller was again before the court and fined £100 and given two years in prison.

The price to pay

The Irish Parliament was persuaded to back Britain's interests in the American War of Independence, but at a hefty price. In the summer of 1776, members of the Dublin legislature voted 99-49 to condemn the actions of the American patriots, many of them Ulster Presbyterians, in filing for independence. The move led to the creation of 22 new Irish peerages and eight promotions for those already in the peerage.

The London Government of King George III followed this up with payments of £11,000 a year in new pensions for forty "well-placed" people who could ensure a proper majority in the new Irish parliament to be elected later that year.

Trade concessions for Ireland were also approved, including the right to export directly the clothing and equipment needed by Crown troops, along with the eligibility of Irish ships in return for considerable bounties. In 1778, Ireland was further authorised to export a large quantities of goods directly to overseas British colonies, including North America.

Resolutely Defending the Frontier

Pittsburgh or Fort Pitt in western Pennsylvania was an isolated frontier outpost during the Revolutionary War and the Scots-Irish
Presbyterian settlers were amongst the most gallant in defence of the
region. The militias were led by Aeneas Mackay and John Gibson - two
men with Ulster roots and a young boy from the same diaspora
Ebenezer Denny was chosen to plant the American flag of independence
on the height of the Yorktown battlements.

In 1776 the Eighth Pennsylvania Line, with Mackay as its colonel,
was formed by order of the Continental Congress to defend the exposed
western border against Indian attack.

The fight for survival by the hardy Scots-Irish settlers on the
Pennsylvanian frontier in the late 1770s is vividly capsuled in poignant
prose from a William G. Lytle, published in a Pittsburgh newspaper.

*"In the winter of 1776-77 Fort Pitt was on the frontier, 30 days from
headquarters and 24 hours from the red death.*

*Washington needed help. The Eighth Pennsylvania Regiment of the
Continental Line started across the mountains in the dead of winter. They
left camp at Kittanning, Jan.6, 1777. Colonel Aeneas Mackay walked at
the head of the line, an old Scotchman, wracked by the cold, but driven by a
fire within.*

*Long days of floundering through the drifts. At night, camp fires burned
in the silent forest places while half -frozen men foraged firewood. They slept
with their hunger, while the wind moaned through the creaking trees.*

*A slow moving column, a dark shadow on the white expanse of snow,
trudging down great mountain passes beneath the stare of a cold sun. A few
black specks far ahead and behind, rangers on the watch for ambush.
Tracking down valleys. Struggling up mountain sides. Ringed by a vast
silence.*

*It was an army without banner and drums. The wild wind clutched at
ragged clothing. The drums of their spirit beat a rally.*

*They trooped down upon the Eastern plains like a company of wild men.
And Colonel Mackay, who had brought them through to Washington, died
soon after he had reported the command.*

The cold had sapped his life away."

30

An American view *of the backwoodsmen of the Alleghenies*

"Along the western frontier of the colonies that were so soon to be the United States, among the foothills of the Alleghenies, on the slopes of the wooded mountains, and in the long trough-like valleys that lay between the ranges, dwelt a peculiar and characteristically American people.

"These frontier folk, the people of the up-country, or back-country, who lived near and among the forest-clad mountains, far away from the long-settled districts of flat coastal plan and sluggish tidal river, were known to themselves and to others as backwoodsmen.

"They all bore a strong likeness to one another in their habits of thought and ways of living, and differed markedly from the people of the older and more civilised communities to the eastward. The western border of the country was then formed by the great-barrier chains of the Alleghenies, which ran north and south from Pennsylvania, through Maryland, Virginia and Carolina, the trend of the valleys being parallel to the sea-coast and the mountains rising highest to the southward.

"It was difficult to cross the ranges from east to west, but it was both easy and natural to follow the valleys between. From Fort Pitt to the high hill-homes of the Cherokees this great tract of wooded and mountainous country possessed nearly the same features and characteristics, differing utterly in physical aspect from the alluvial plains bordering the ocean.

"So likewise, the backwoods mountaineers who dwelt near the great watershed that separates the Atlantic stream, from the springs of the Watauga, the Kanawha and the Monongahela were all cast in the same mould and resembled much more than any of them did their immediate neighbors of the plains.

"The backwoodsmen of Pennsylvania had little in common with the peaceful population of Quakers and Germans who lived between the Delaware and the Susquehanna and their near kinsmen of the Blue Ridge and the Great Smoky Mountains were separated by an equally wide gulf from the aristocratic planter communities that flourished in the tide-water regions of Virginia and the Carolinas.

"Near the coast the lines of division between the colonies corresponded fairly well with the differences between the populations; but after striking the foothills, though the political boundaries continued to go east and west, those both of ethnic and of physical significance began to run north and south.

"The backwoodsmen were Americans by birth and parentage, and of mixed race; but the dominant strain in their blood was that of Presbyterian Irish - the Scotch-Irish, as they were often called.

"Full credit had been awarded the Roundhead and the Cavalier for their leadership in our history; nor have we been altogether blind to the deeds of the Hollander and the Huguenot, but it is doubtful if we have fully realised the importance of the part played by that stern and virile people, the Irish whose preachers taught the creed of John Knox and John Calvin.

"These Irish representatives of the Convenanters were in the west almost what the Puritans were in the north-east and more than the Cavaliers were in the south. Mingled with descendants of many other races, they nevertheless formed the kernel of the distinctively and intensely American stock who were the pioneers of our people in their march westwards, the vanguard of the army of fighting settlers, who with axe and rifle won their way from the Alleghenies to the Rio Grande and the Pacific.

"The Presbyterian Irish were themselves already a mixed people. Though mainly descended from Scotch ancestors - who came originally from both lowlands and highlands, from among both the Scotch Saxons and the Scotch Celts - many of them were of English, a few of French Huguenot, and quite a number of the true old Misesian Irish extradition.

"They were the Protestants of the Protestants; they detested the Catholics, whom they had conquered, and regarded the Episcopalians by whom they themselves had been oppressed, with a more sullen, but scarcely less intense hatred.

"They were a truculent and obstinate people, and gloried in the warlike renown of their forefathers, the men who had followed Cromwell, and who had shared in the defence of Derry and in the victories of the Boyne and Aughrim.

"They did not begin to come to America in any numbers till after the opening of the 18th century; by 1730 they were fairly swarming across the ocean, for the most part in two streams, the larger going to the port of Philadelphia, the smaller to Charleston.

"Pushing through the long settled lowlands of the seacoast, they at once made their abode at the foot of the mountains and became the outposts of civilisation. From Pennsylvania, wither the great majority of them had come, they drifted south along the foothills and down the long valleys, till they met their brethren from Charleston, who had pushed up into the Carolina back-country.

"In this land of hills, covered by unbroken forest, they took root and flourished, stretching in a broad belt from north to south, a shield of sinewy men thrust in between the people of the seaboard and the red warriors of the wilderness.

"All through this region they were alike; as they had so little kinship with the Cavalier as with the Quaker; the West was won by those who have been rightly called the Roundheads of the south, the same men, who, before any others declared for American Independence.

"The two facts of most importance to remember in dealing with our pioneer history are, first, that the western portions of Virginia and the Carolinas were people by an entirely different stock from that which had long existed in the tide-water regions of these colonies, and, secondly, except for those in the Carolinas who came from Charleston, the immigrants of this stock were mostly from the north, from the great breeding ground and nursery in western Pennsylvania.

"That these Irish Presbyterians were a bold and hardy race is proved by their at once pushing past the settled regions, and plunging into the wilderness as the leaders of the white advance. They were the first and last set of immigrants to do this; all others have merely followed in the wake of their predecessors. But indeed, they were fitted to be Americans from the very start.

"They were kinsfolk of the Covenanters; they deemed it a religious duty to interpret their own Bible, and held for a divine right the election of their own clergy.

For generations their whole ecclesiastic and scholastic systems had been fundamentally democratic. In the hard life of the frontier they lost much of their religion, and they had but scant opportunity to give their children the schooling in which they believed; but what few meeting-houses and school-houses there were on the borders were theirs.

"The numerous families of colonial English who came among them adopted their religion if they adopted any. The creed of the backwoodsmen who had a creed at all was Presbyterianism; for the Episcopacy of the tide-water lands obtained no foothold in the mountains, and the Methodists and Baptists had just begun to appear in the west when the Revolution broke out."

**- PRESIDENT THEODORE ROOSEVELT,
from his book The Winning of the West.**

Seventeen American Presidents
with Ulster links

ANDREW JACKSON: (Democrat 1829-37). Born 1767 in the Waxhaws region of North Carolina, his parents left Ulster in 1765, having lived in the village of Boneybefore near Carrickfergus, Co. Antrim. Andrew, a lawyer, helped draft the constitution for Tennessee, which set up as the 16th state of the Union in 1796. He was victorious US commander at the Battle of New Orleans in 1815.

★

JAMES KNOX POLK: (Democrat 1845-49). Born 1795 near Charlotte in North Carolina, he was descended from a Robert Polk (Pollock) of Londonderry, who arrived in the American colonies about 1680. Was a Governor of Tennessee and he and his wife Sarah are buried in Nashville. A kinsman signed the Mecklenburg Declaration of May, 1775 which preceded the Declaration of Independence.

JAMES BUCHANAN: (Democrat 1857-61). Born 1791 in Mercersburg, Pennsylvania, James Buchanan was a Presbyteiran like his Presidential predecessors Jackson and Polk. The family originated from Deroran near Omagh, Co. Tyrone and left Donegal for America in 1783. Buchanan was the only bachelor President. Buchanan once declared: "My Ulster blood is my most priceless heritage."

★

ANDREW JOHNSON: (Democrat 1865-69). Born 1808 in Raleigh, North Carolina. His Presbyterian namesake and grandfather from Mounthill outside Larne in Co. Antrim came to America about 1750. Johnson rose to the Presidency from humble log cabin origins and he worked as a tailor for many years. He was Mayor of Greeneville in Tennessee, Governor of Tennessee and Vice-President to Abraham Lincoln before assuming the Presidency on Lincoln's assassination.

ULYSSES SIMPSON GRANT: (Republican 1869-77). Born 1822 in Point Pleasant, Ohio. Grant, also of Presbyterian stock, successfully commanded the Union Army in the American Civil War. His mother Hannah Simpson was descended from the Simpson family of Dergenagh near Dungannon, Co. Tyrone. His great grandfather, John Simpson, left Ulster for America in 1760. President Grant was a Methodist.

CHESTER ALAN ARTHUR: (Republican 1881-85). Born 1830 in Fairfield, Vermont, his grandfather and father, Baptist pastor William Arthur, emigrated to the United States from Dreen near Cullybackey, Co. Antrim in 1801. He was Vice President to President James A. Garfield and became President on Garfield's assassination in 1881.

★

GROVER CLEVELAND: (Democrat 1885-89 and 1893-97). Born 1837 in Caldwell, New Jersey. His maternal grandfather Abner Neal left Co. Antrim in the late 18th century. He was the son of a Presbyterian minister and before becoming President was a lawyer.

★

BENJAMIN HARRISON: (Republican 1889-90). Born 1833 at North Bend, Ohio. Two of his great grandfathers James Irwin and William McDowell were Ulstermen. President Harrison was a devout Presbyterian and fought in the Civil War on the Union side.

★

WILLIAM McKINLEY: (Republican 1897-1901). Born 1843 in Niles, Ohio. A Presbyterian, he was the great grandson of James McKinley, who emigrated to America from Conagher near Ballymoney, Co. Antrim about 1743. He was assassinated at Buffalo, New York on September 6, 1901.

★

THEODORE ROOSEVELT: (Republican 1905-09). Born 1858 in New York City. President Roosevelt, who wrote admiringly of the courage and exploits of the Scots-Irish, is believed to have Presbyterian ancestors on his maternal side from Larne, Co. Antrim. Folklore in East Antrim link him to the Irvines of Carneac near Larne and the Bullochs from the same area. Roosevelt belonged to the Dutch Reformed Church.

★

WOODROW WILSON: (Democrat 1913-21). Born 1856 in Staunton, Virginia. He was grandson of James Wilson, who emigrated to North Carolina from Dergelt near Strabane, Co. Tyrone. His father, the Rev. Dr. Joseph Ruffles Wilson, was a Presbyterian minister and Woodrow was a lecturer at Princeton College before becoming President.

★

HARRY TRUMAN: (Democrat 1949-53). Born 1884 at Lamar, Missouri. His maternal grandfather, Solomon Young was of Scots-Irish settler stock and moved from Kentucky to Kansas City,

Missouri in 1840. President Truman was a Baptist, but he attended the Presbyterian church as a youth.

RICHARD MILLHOUSE NIXON: (Republican 1969-74). Born 1913 in Yorba Linda, California, he had Ulster connections on two sides of his family. His Nixon Presbyterian ancestors (the family of James Nixon) left Co. Antrim for the Delaware region in the mid-18th century, while the Millhouses came from Carrickfergus and Ballymoney also in Co. Antrim. Richard Nixon was a Quaker.

JAMES EARL CARTER: (Democrat 1977-81). Born 1924 in Plains, Georgia. Scots-Irish settler Andrew Cowan, believed to come from Co. Antrim, was the great grandfather of President Carter's great grandfather on his mother's side. Cowan, a Presbyterian, was one of the first settlers at Boonesborough in the South Carolina Piedmont region in 1772. Jimmy Carter is a Baptist.

GEORGE BUSH: (Republican 1989-93). Born 1924 at Milton, Massachusetts. An ancestor on his mother's side was William Gault, who was born in Ulster (very probably Co. Antrim) and with his wife Margaret were first settlers of Tennessee in 1796, living in Blount County. President Bush is an Episcopalian.

WILLIAM JEFFERSON CLINTON: (Democrat 1993-2001). Born 1946 in Hope Hempstead County, Arkansas. President Clinton claims to be a relative of Lucas Cassidy, who left Co. Fermanagh for America around 1750. Lucas Cassidy was of Presbyterian stock. President Bill Clinton is a Baptist.

GEORGE W. BUSH: (Republican 2001-). born 1946 in Texas. President Bush, son of President George Walker Bush, is descended on his father's maternal side from the late 18th century East

Tennessee settler William Gault, who was born in the North of Ireland (very probably Co. Antrim).

★

Vice-President

JOHN C. CALHOUN (Democrat 1825-32). Son of a Co. Donegal Presbyterian father Patrick Calhoun and mother Margaret Caldwell, who was Virginia-born of Co. Antrim immigrant parents, this eminent South Carolina statesman was Vice President to President John Quincy Adams and President Andrew Jackson.

• Presidents Andrew Johnson, Chester Alan Arthur and Richard Millhouse Nixon also served terms as Vice-Presidents.

★★★

American Presidential Seal

Author's *acknowledgments*

- Professor George Schweitzer, Tennessee State University, Knoxville
- Dr John Rice-Irwin, Museum of Appalachia, Norris, Tennessee
- Kent Whiteworth, East Tennessee Historical Society, Knoxville
- Cherel Henderson, East Tennessee Historical Society, Knoxville
- David Wright (artist), Gallatin, Tennessee
- Christine Johnston (Librarian), Ulster-American Folk Park, Omagh, Co Tyrone
- Lord John Laird of Artigarvan, Ulster-Scots Agency, Belfast
- Staff at McClung Museum, Knoxville, Tennessee
- Alan McMillan, Irish Presbyterian Historical Department, Belfast
- Peter McKitterick, US Consulate General, Belfast
- Mark T. Esper and Jayson Roehl, Professional Staff Members, US Senate, Washington D.C.
- Dr Bobbie Moss, Blacksburg, South Carolina
- Ulster-Scots Agency, Belfast

Pictures *and illustrations*

- David Wright (artist), Gallatin, Tennessee
- East Tennessee Historical Society, Knoxville
- Dover Publications Inc, Mineola, New York (The American Revolution: A Picture Sourcebook by John Grafton)
- Bellerophon Books, Santa Barbara, California
- Robert Windsor Wilson (artist), Wooruff, South Carolina
- United States Embassy, London
- United States Consulate General, Belfast
- United States Senate Photographic Studio, Washington D.C.
- Thomas Gilcrease, Institute of American History and Arts, Tulsa, Oklahoma
- Tennessee State Museum, Nashville.
- The National Trust, Northern Ireland

Bibliography *and references consulted*

- The Scotch-Irish: A Social History by James G. Leyburn
- Early Scotch Contributions to the United States by T. J. Werterbaker
- Puritanism and Democracy by Ralph Barton Perry
- The American Irish and their Influence on Irish Politics by Philip H. Bagenal
- First Families of Tennessee (East Tennessee Historical Society publication 2000)
- The Great Wagon Road by Parke Rouse Jun.
- America's War of Independence 1763-1783 (Concise Illustrated History)
- The American Revolution: An American Sourcebook by John Grafton
- The Cousins' War by Kevin Philips
- Albion's Seed by David Hackett Fischer
- The Life of Andrew Jackson by Robert V. Remini
- With Fire and Sword: The Battle of Kings Mountain 1780 by Wilma Dykeman
- Encyclopedia of the American Revolution by Mark M. Boatner 111
- Signers of the Declaration by Katherine and John Bakeless
- Ireland and Irishmen in American War of Independence by Academy Press, Dublin
- Ireland, Irishmen and Revolutionary America by David Noel Doyle
- Irish Historical Studies: The Scotch-Irish and the Revolution in North Carolina by E. R. R. Green
- A Defence of the Revolutionary History of North Carolina by J. S. Jones
- The British Isles and the War of American Independence by Stephen Conway
- In Pursuit of Equal Liberty: George Bryan and the Revolution in Pennsylvania by Joseph S. Foster
- John Peebles' American War 1776-1782 by Ira D. Gruber
- The Overmountain Men by Pat Alderman
- One Heroic Hour at Kings Mountain by Pat Alderman
- Patriots of Kings Mountain by Dr Bobby Gilmer Moss
- Land of the Free: Ulster and the American Revolution by Ronnie Hanna
- Scottish-Irish Contributions to Early American Life and Culture by William C. Lehmann

- Kate Barry by Mary Montgomery Miller
- History of Nazarath Presbyterian Church, Moore, South Carolina
- The Ulster-Scot by James B. Woodbourne
- The Scotch-Irish (The Scot in North Britain, North Ireland and North America) by Charles A. Hanna
- From Sea to Shining Sea by James Alexander Thom
- Tennessee - the Backcountry Era - (Tennessee Historical Quarterly)
- The Valley of Virginia in the American Revolution by F. H. Hart
- The Scotch-Irish in America by John Walker Dinsmore
- The Winning of the West by President Theodore Roosevelt
- The Scotch-Irish in America by Henry Jones Ford
- The Scotch-Irish of Colonial Pennsylvania by Wayland F. Dunaway
- The Mecklenburg Signers and their Neighbours by Woreth S. Ray
- Heroes of the American Revolution by David Brownell
- George Washington's War: The Saga of the American Revolution by Robert Leckie
- To the Best of My Ability: The American Presidents - edited by James McPherson
- The Road to Guilford Courthouse (The American Revolution in the Carolinas) by John Buchanan
- Battle of Boyd's Creek, Appalachian Life and Old State of Franklin
- Orgins of the American Revolution by John C. Miller
- The Wataugans by Max Dixon
- Carolina Cradle: Settlement of Northwest Carolina Frontier by Robert W. Ramsey
- American Scripture: How American Declared its Independence from Britain by Pauline Maier
- First Presbyterian Church, Pittsburgh, Pennsylvania.
- History of Philadelphia (Schart and Westcott 1884)

Index

Declaration of 13 United States of America - in Congress, Philadelphia, July 4, 1776

"When in the course of human events, it becomes necessary for one people to dissolve the political bands which have connected them with another, and to assume among the powers of the earth, the separate and equal station to which the laws of nature and of nature's God entitled them, a decent respect to the opinions of mankind requires they should declare the causes which impel them to the separation.

"We hold these truths to be self-evident, that all men are created equal, that they are endowed by their Creator with certain unalienable rights, that among these are life, liberty and the pursuit of happiness.

"That to secure these rights, governments are instituted among men, deriving their just powers from the consent of the governed, that whenever any form of government becomes destructive of these ends, it is the right of the people to alter or to abolish it, and to institute a new government, laying its foundation on such principles and organising its powers in such form, as to them shall seem most likely to effect their safety and happiness.

"Prudence, indeed, will dictate that governments long established should not be changed for light and transient causes, and, accordingly, all experience hath shown, that mankind are more disposed to suffer, while evils are sufferable, than to right themselves by abolishing the forms to which they are accustomed. But when a long train of abuses and usurpations, pursuing invariably the same object evinces a design to reduce them under absolute despotism, it is their right, it is their duty, to throw of such government, and to provide new guards for their future security.

"Such has been the patient sufferance of these Colonies, and such is now the necessity which constrains them to alter their former systems of government. The history of the present King of Great Britain (George 111) is a history of repeated injuries and usurpations, all having in direct object the establishment of an absolute tyranny over these states.

To prove this let facts be submitted to a candid world:

- He has refused his assent to laws, the most wholesome and necessary for the public good.
- He has forbidden his governors to pass laws of immediate and pressing importance, unless suspended in their operation till his assent should be obtained, and when so suspended, he has utterly neglected to attend to them.

- He has refused to pass other laws for the accommodation of large districts of people, unless those people would relinquish the right of representation in the legislature, a right inestimable to them and formidable to tyrants only.
- He has abdicated government here, by declaring us out of his Protection and destroyed the lives of our people.
- He has plundered our seas, ravaged our coasts, burnt our towns and destroyed the lives of our people.
- He has excited domestic insurrections amongst us.

"In every stage of these oppressions we have petitioned for redress in the most humble terms. Our repeated petitions have been answered by repeated injury. A prince, whose character is thus marked by every act which may define a tyrant, is unfit to be the ruler of a free people.

"Nor have we been wanting in attentions to our British brethren. We have warned them from time to time of attempts by their leglislation to extend an unwarrantable jurisdiction over us. We have reminded them of the circumstances of our emigration and settlement here. We have appealed to their native justice and magnanimity and we have conjured them by the ties of our common kindred to disavow these usurpations, which, would inevitably interrupt our connections and correspondence.

"They too have been deaf to the voice of justice and, of consanguinity. We must, therefore, acquiesce in the necessity, which denounces our separation and hold them, as we hold the rest of mankind, enemies in war, in peace friends.

"We therefore, the representatives of the United States of America in general Congress, assembled, appealing to the Supreme Judge of the world for the rectitude of our intentions, do, in the name, and by authority of the good people of these colonies, solemnly publish and declare that these united colonies are, and of right, ought to be free and independent states: that they are absolved from allegiance to the British Crown, and that all political connections between them and the state of Great Britain, is and ought to be totally dissolved.

"And that as free and independent states, they have full power to levy war, conclude peace, contract alliances, establish commerce and to do all other acts of things which independent states may of right do. And for the support of this Declaration, with a firm reliance on the protection of Divine Providence, we mutually pledge to each other our lives, our fortunes and our sacred honor."

THE SCOTS-IRISH CHRONICLES
by Billy Kennedy

THE SCOTS-IRISH IN THE HILLS OF TENNESSEE
(First published 1995)

This book, centred in Tennessee, is the definite story of how the American frontier of the late 18th century was advanced and the indomitable spirit of the Scots-Irish shines through on every page. From the Great Smoky Mountain region to the Cumberland Plateau and the Mississippi delta region, the Scots-Irish created a civilisation out of a wilderness. The inheritance they left was hard-won, but something to cherish. The careers of Tennessean Presidents Andrew Jackson, James Knox Polk and Andrew Johnson and state luminaries Davy Crockett and Sam Houston are catalogued in the book.

THE SCOTS-IRISH IN THE SHENANDOAH VALLEY
(First published 1996)

The beautiful Shenandoah Valley alongside the majestic backdrop of the Blue Ridge Mountains of Virginia is the idyllic setting for the intriguing story of a brave resolute people who tamed the frontier. The Ulster-Scots were a breed of people who could move mountains. They did this literally with their bare hands in regions like the Shenandoah Valley, winning the day for freedom and liberty of conscience in the United States. In the Shenandoah Valley, the Scots-Irish led the charge for the American patriots in the Revolutionary War and for the Confederates in the Civil War almost a century later.

THE SCOTS-IRISH IN THE CAROLINAS
(First published 1997)

The Piedmont areas of the Carolinas, North and South, were settled by tens of thousands of Scots-Irish Presbyterians in the second half of the 18th century. Some moved down the Great Wagon Road from Pennsylvania, others headed to the up-country after arriving at the port of Charleston. The culture, political heritage and legacy of the Scots-Irish so richly adorned the fabric of American life and the Carolinas was an important homeland for many of these people. It was also the launching pad for the long trek westwards to new lands and the fresh challenge of the expanding frontier.

THE SCOTS-IRISH IN PENNSYLVANIA AND KENTUCKY
(First published 1998)

Pennsylvania and Kentucky are two American states settled primarily at opposite ends of the 18th century by Ulster-Scots Presbyterians, yet this book details how the immigrant trail blended in such diverse regions. William Penn and the Quaker community encouraged the European settlers to move in large numbers to the colonial lands in Pennsylvania from the beginning of the 18th century and the Scots-Irish were the earliest settlers to set up homes in cities like Philadelphia and Pittsburgh. Kentucky, established as a state in 1792, was pioneered by Ulster-Scots families who moved through the Cumberland Gap and down the Wilderness Road with English explorer Daniel Boone.

★★★

FAITH AND FREEDOM: THE SCOTS-IRISH IN AMERICA
(First published 1999)

A common thread runs through Pennsylvania, Virginia, North Carolina, South Carolina, Tennessee, West Virginia, Georgia, Kentucky, Alabama and other Appalachian neighbourings states - that of a settlement of people who had firmly set their faces on securing for all time - their Faith and Freedom. This inspirational journey on the Scots-Irish Presbyterian settlers details how they moved the American frontier to its outer limits, founding log cabin churches that were to spiral the message of the gospel, and establishing schools, which were to expand into some of the foremost educational institutions in the United States.

★★★

HEROES OF THE SCOTS-IRISH IN AMERICA
(First published 2000)

Heroism was a distinct characteristic of the 18th century Scots-Irish immigrants and the raw courage shown by these dogged, determined people in very difficult circumstances helped make the United States great. Forging a civilisation out of a wilderness was a real challenge for the Ulster settlers and how well they succeeded in moulding a decent law-abiding society, from the eastern seaboard states, through the Appalachian region into the south to Texas and beyond. The Scots-Irish heroes, and heroines have become enshrined in American history, not just Presidents, statesmen, soldiers, and churchmen, but many plain ordinary citizens whose quiet, unselfish deeds were worthy of note, and a shining example to others.

These books are available from authorised booksellers in the United Kingdom, the United States and the Republic of Ireland or direct from the publishers in Belfast (Northern Ireland) and Greenville (South Carolina).

Scots-Irish lectures delivered in United States by the author 1994-2001

TENNESSEE

- Middle Tennessee State University, Murfreesboro
- East Tennessee State University, Johnson City
- Belmont University, Nashville
- Maryville College, Blount County
- Kings's Presbytterian College, Bristol
- University of Tennessee, Chattanooga
- Tennessee State University, Chattanooga
- Tennessee Historical Society, Nashville
- East Tennessee Historical Society, Knoxville
- Chattanooga Historical Society
- The Hermitage, Nashville
- Tolahoma Historical Socuiety
- Scottish Association, Knockville
- Sycamore Shoals State Historic Park, Elizabethton
- Rotary Club, Rogersville
- Museum of Appalachia, Norris
- Rotary Club, Morristown
- Library, Greeneville
- Zion Presbyterian Church, Columbia , Maury County
- Tennessee 'First Families' Reunion (2000), Knoxville)
- Jefferson County Historical Society, Dandridge
- Jonesboro Visitors Centre and Museum
- Louden County Historical Socieity, Leinore City
- Sullivan County Genealogical Society, Kingsport
- Cumberland County Genealogical and Historical Society, Crossville.

VIRGINIA

- Museum of American Frontier Culture, Straunton
- Ferrum College
- Grayson County Historical Society, Independence
- Roanoke Historical Society
- Abingdon Historical Society
- The Bookery, Lexington

- Woodrow Wilson Birthplace and Museum, Staunton
- Book Store, Charlottsville
- Harrisonburg/Rockingham Historical Society
- Richmond Historical Society

KENTUCKY

- Berea College, Berea
- Cumberland Gap National Historical Park, Middlesboro

SOUTH CAROLINA

- Clemson University
- McCormick County Historoical Society
- Donalds Historical, Boonesborough
- Honea Path School, Donalds
- Greenville Presbyterian Church
- Erskine Theological College
- Gaffney College
- Kings Mountain National Military Park

NORTH CAROLINA

- Historical Society, Franklin
- Andrew Jackson Centre, Waxhaws,
- Appalacian Conference, Boone
- Historical Society, Waynesville

PENNSYLVANIA

- Scotch-Irish Society of the United States, Philadelphia
- Elizabethton College
- Donegal Presbyterian Church, Lancaster County
- First Pittsburgh Presbyterian Church
- Historical Cultural Centre, Winter's House, Elizabethton

ALABAMA

- Tennessee Valley Historical Society, Huntsville